# STOCK MARKET RULES

# STOCK MARKET RULES

## 50 of the Most Widely Held Investment Axioms Explained, Examined, and Exposed

**THIRD EDITION**

**Michael D. Sheimo**

**McGraw-Hill**

New York  Chicago  San Francisco  Lisbon
London  Madrid  Mexico City  Milan  New Delhi
San Juan  Seoul  Singapore  Sidney  Toronto

1 2 3 4 5 6 7 8 9 0   FGR/FGR   0 9 8 7 6 5 4

ISBN 0-07-144587-0

 This book is printed on recycled, acid-free paper containing a minimum of 50% recycled de-inked paper.

**Library of Congress Cataloging-in-Publication Data**

Sheimo, Michael D., 1944-
    Stock market rules : 50 of the most widely held investment axioms explained, examined, and exposed / by Michael D. Sheimo.— 3rd ed.
        p. cm.
    ISBN 0-07-144587-0 (pbk. : alk. paper)
    1. Investments—Miscellanea. 2. Stock exchanges—Miscellanea. I. Title.
HG4521.S519 2004
332.63'22—dc22                                                                2004015435

*For Linda, a rule I will always follow.*

# CONTENTS

# PREFACE

Axioms relating to the stock market have probably been around as long as stock trading. One of the oldest known axioms relates to selling short: *He who sells what isn't hisen must buy it back or go to prison.* The continuous buying and selling in the stock market attracts clever sayings and words of wisdom about what to do or what not to do in a particular situation. Always remember that buying or selling stock involves two differences of opinion. The buyers believe that the price will rise and the sellers believe the price is going nowhere or down. How can axioms about trading stock be helpful? They are based on real stock market experience, and experience is often the seasoning that makes investors richer or poorer.

Many old axioms are still true today, while others that were once true have changed. "Buy on Monday, Sell on Friday" (Chapter 25) is a well-known principle among investors, but many aren't aware that the patter has changed. Statistically, the axiom is not as good a strategy as it was prior to 1990.

"Good Companies Buy Their Own Stock" (Chapter 3) might be good for the company, but is it always good for the investor? Bellwethers—stocks that turn before the rest of the market—have been kicked around for decades. Part of the problem with bellwethers is their tendency to be inconsistent, turning ahead of the market sometimes or with and after the market other times, as shown in Chapter 5, "Watch the Bellwethers."

Although many of the time-honored sayings are helpful, knowledge of the axiom alone is not enough; it is essential to understand the meaning behind the saying. If it is better to "Sell the Losers and Let the Winners Run" (Chapter 15), how does an investor determine which stock is a loser and which one is a winner? Is price the only determining factor, or should other factors be considered? If the investor continually sells the losers, how and when does profit taking become an event? Answers to questions like these can give the investor a strong understanding of the full meaning behind the axiom. These are only a few of the concepts covered in this book. A review of the Contents pages will give a complete picture.

The one thing certain in the stock market is change. But sometimes the old can become new again. The term "new economy" was popular to describe tech and Internet stocks, whereas the companies that had been around for decades became known as the "old economy stocks." Most of these new economy stocks became referred to as "the tech bubble" as they came crashing down. Many of the old then resumed their label of "Blue Chip" stocks.

A look at the list of illustrations shows the depth of coverage of this comprehensive work. The book contains many charts of stock market indexes and individual stock prices. Although the analysis is relevant to the time of the charts, things change. In today's market, change happens quickly. The price charts and analyses are not meant to be current buy or sell recommendations; rather they show real-world examples of the concepts presented in the book.

The "rules" presented in this book are axioms based on investing in and trading stocks of publicly held corporations. The concepts are explained, examined, and exposed in order to bring about an understanding of the many fine points of stock trading. The investor's understanding of these concepts will improve his or her decision-making process and help him or her with the buying and selling of stocks. Greater knowledge and understanding can lead to greater profits.

What's the future of the stock market? "It's Always a Bull Market" (Chapter 6). Once the major powers of the world settle down and get back to the war of business instead of the business of war, we'll be in for some major economic surprises. Development in countries like China, Russia, and India could open up amazing markets for all sorts of products and services. The one commodity these countries have is people and people need things. As stability and growth materialize, people will demand better standards of living, better products, and better services. It's inevitable. It is this kind of demand that creates earnings and higher stock prices.

# PART I

# Research

To say that research is important to investing is like saying air is important to breathing. The strange thing is that research is often overlooked by the amateur and the professional alike. Instead they look for today's action. What's moving? Where's it going?

Ideally, the investor knows ahead of time what's likely to be moving, where's it going, and why. To have a relatively small group of stocks that one follows well is both wise and often fruitful. If following the group is not fruitful, change the makeup. Find different stocks to follow.

Getting the basic information before the investment is made can do absolute wonders for saving the investor money. A sudden price increase should never be the only reason to buy a stock. An increase in either price or volume might call your attention to a particular company, but also get the background on what's happening.

In recent times one only need look at the fortunes of WorldCom or Enron to see the disaster that can befall an investor who has little or no understanding of a company. There are still people who got burned on both of these stocks who have very little knowledge of what the companies did and what happened to them.

Do the research before you invest, not after.

# CHAPTER 1

# Get Information Before You Invest, Not After

**M**ost of the complicated aspects of our lives could be improved by gathering information before taking action. Asking why and digging deeper for information is an inconvenience because it calls for analysis, thought, and the formation of a conclusion. These activities take time and energy, and they can often lead to confusion and frustration. To avoid these problems, we mainly depend on the wisdom of others or adopt a shoot-from-the-hip approach to investing.

Depending entirely on the wisdom of others or shooting from the hip can lead to many misunderstandings. Misunderstandings cause bad timing and poor strategies. Investment advice can be helpful, but it can be even more useful as a point of reference, a second opinion, rather than being accepted as the only approach.

In the stock market, the odds of doing well are improved for the investor who becomes familiar with the current action of the market and the particular stock of interest. Becoming familiar with the action can be accomplished by asking why: Why is the market making this move? Why is the stock an attractive purchase now?

## MARKET MOVES

The stock market is a continuous auction, with the same product being bought and sold every business day. If there are more buyers than sellers, the market and prices of individual stocks rise. If there are more sellers than buyers, prices fall. It's that simple.

But if it's so simple, then why does it seem so complicated? Why are all these investors buying and selling stock? If they're investors, shouldn't they all be buying and holding stock for its investment value? Why are people surprised when the stock market drops a few hundred points? Does a severe market correction mean the economy will take a nosedive? The newscasters always say the stock market forecasts the economic situation six months to a year away. So what gives?

## Anticipation

The most important fact to remember is that the stock market always trades in anticipation of future events. Often, investors are looking ahead six to 12 months, but (and here's the kicker) not always. If the Dow Industrial Average is down 50 points or more, the major, professional investors couldn't care less about what might happen in six to 12 months. They are concerned only with what might happen in the more immediate future, that being the next 10 minutes. The faster the market drops, the shorter their focus becomes. The believers of doom and gloom busily pat themselves on the back for being correct, and those who know better take a more moderate stance. Thankfully, it usually takes more than an over-correction in the market to cause an economic recession.

## Real, Imagined, and Fabricated Factors

A real factor motivating stock market buyers or sellers is money—specifically, the availability of money. Money availability, as it changes with a movement of the interest rates or the earnings of corporations.

An imagined factor can be the respected opinion of an economist or market analyst as to the current strength or weakness of the stock market.

A fabricated factor is the merciless hammering of computerized sell programs. The sells are often implemented with the intent of testing market strength by pushing the market down as far as possible. "As far as possible" is a point that is reached when buyers enter the scene and stop the decline; that point is called *support.*

On June 2, 2001, these factors came into play and made a turn in the Primary Trend of the Dow Industrial Average and other major indexes. The Dow dropped 3,101 points before reaching support and starting the recovery. It did a retracement to the 10,635 level, turned and started down again, this time dropping to the 7,423 point level (Figure 1-1).

## FIGURE 1-1

Dow Industrial Average, April 2001–February 2004

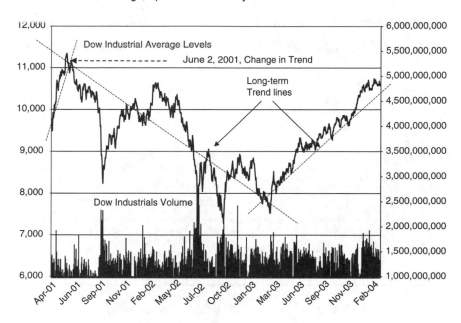

## Dow Industrial Average, 2001 to 2004

Investors who noticed the turn in the stock market by observing the daily decline in the Dow Industrial and Transportation Averages, and who listened to the market opinions given by many analysts before June, would likely have taken some protective action. Market anticipation had been fueled by interest in tech stocks. Once the tech stock bubble came to a sudden halt, so did the market rally. The market correction was more severe than expected due to strong selling effects of programmed trading. Some would say the market became oversold, as shown by a quick recovery.

## Nasdaq and Standard & Poor's 500 Indexes

These indexes (Figure 1-2) performed a similar maneuver, turning, going flat, and then starting a downtrend. All three indexes showed a similar trend, with frequent secondary rallies. All three groups of stocks turned and crossed the trend line in the fall of 2002. The following year had a strong uptrend for the majority of stocks.

## FIGURE 1–2

Nasdaq Composite Index and S&P 500 Index, 1999-2003

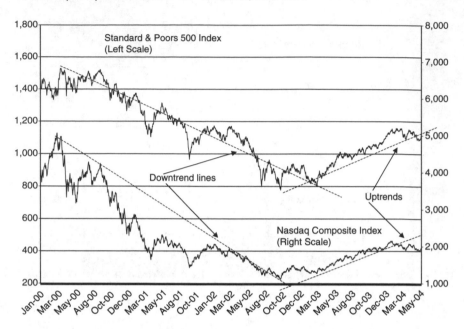

## STOCK MOVES: DOWN

Buying a car, a computer, or a new television, only to see it on sale the following week, can be a big source of irritation. Of course, the same holds true for stocks. To pay $52 a share one day, then to hear some negative news and see a price of $42 the next week, is not a pleasant experience. If the investor's research and selection are valid, the price will probably recover and move to new highs. But the price damage on the way down can be difficult to endure. An interesting phenomenon can occur with a stock price that appears to keep on dropping.

As the price declines, investors will appear to buy up shares at perceived bargain prices. If enough of these bargain hunters appear, they can stop the price drop, but sellers might overpower them. *Bottom* is where the price stops declining and goes flat or begins to retrace its upward trend. The bottom shown in the chart in Figure 1-1 was reached at 7,552.1 in the Dow Industrial Average on March 12, 2003.

### On Sale, Limited Time Only

Many investors consider a market "dip," "pullback," "correction," or "bear market" a buying opportunity. The price is lower, the stock's on sale. The reasons for a price decline can be serious; lower earnings or estimates are predicted, credit ratings are lowered, or a possible lawsuit or tax problem has developed. The reason for a price decline might not be so serious: market correction, profit taking, employee stock distribution, or no news-related reason at all. Whatever the reason for a stock price move, it can be worthwhile to find out why it is moving before investing.

Information about a stock in question can be obtained from the news media, the Internet, or by calling the company directly. Calling the company might be difficult if hundreds of other investors are trying to do the same thing. Often calling the stockbroker or checking a news service on a computer will provide the answer. Learning why a stock is declining in price can enable the investor to form a strategy of buy, hold, or sell.

## STOCK MOVES: SIDEWAYS

Again, ask questions and search for answers. Why isn't the stock price moving? If other similar stocks and the market are doing well, there is a reason for a lack of movement in a given stock. Has there been bad news recently that has created a lack of investor interest, or is the stock currently a gem waiting to be discovered?

Although rare, undiscovered gems can experience dramatic price surges with even a small amount of publicity. Some investors follow a strategy of seeking out these gems, but often they end up with well-run companies that the market doesn't like. Usually they are basically good companies with limited growth potential. Major investors search for companies with virtually unlimited growth potential.

## STOCK MOVES: UPWARD

Why a stock price is moving upward is most important to investors who don't currently own it but would like to be in on the action. Normally, when there is a sudden surge in either the stock market or an individual stock, the news appears quickly to trumpet the event.

## WHEN TO BUY

Some believe that any time is a good time to buy stock, because over the long term, the stock will grow and prosper. Essentially that's correct, although there can obviously be better times than others to buy stock. Usually the best time to buy stock in general is when a downtrend turns up and solidly crosses the trend line. If this is the beginning of a new uptrend and not just a secondary trend, the timing should be good.

# CHAPTER 2

# Price Doubling Is Easy at Low Prices

Many "boiler room" sales representatives have touted this doubtful idea more than once. Yes, it can be easy for some low-priced stocks to double in price. However, it can also be easy for high-priced stocks to double in price. The point is that price doubling depends on factors other than the current price level. For example, it depends on changes in efficiency, restructuring, revenue growth, or earnings growth. The stocks might be new companies or old companies that have recently had earnings problems, companies that show signs of a turnaround.

Like Onyx Acceptance Corporation.

## Onyx

On January 2, 2003, Onyx traded at $2.73. The stock price more than doubled by June, and increased by the same amount by July. It finally topped out at $11.73 by December (Figure 2-1). That kind of growth is terrific for any priced stock, if it stabilizes and doesn't drop back to previous levels.

The big question for the investor is: "Do I get out now or hold on to the stock?" There is no easy answer. No one wants to sell a stock too soon and leave money on the table. At the same time, it can be terribly aggravating to see a stock price double and fall back to previous low levels. Volatility can be an additional frustration. Onyx has a beta factor of 1.0, which means that it is about as volatile as the rest of the stock market.

## FIGURE 2–1

Onyx Acceptance Corporation, January 2003–May 2004

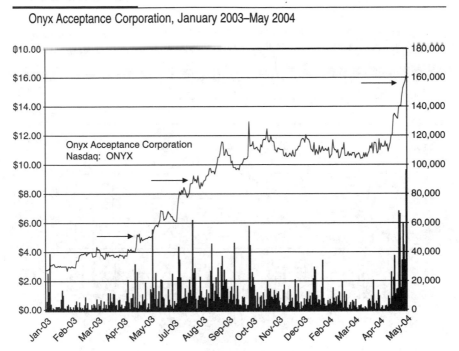

What about a higher-priced stock?

## Texas Instruments

Starting in January 1999, at $22.29 per share, the price doubled by October and nearly doubled again in February 2000 (Figure 2-2). Wow! That's terrific. It's truly amazing to see any stock price double in that short a time. The trouble is, it wasn't stable. As part of the Technology sector, it was a bubble about to burst. The price then fell nearly as fast as it rose. Technology stocks fell and brought the market down with them. The stock trader who got out fast enough made good money. The buy and hold investor became worried and frustrated.

It is interesting to note that Texas Instruments runs a beta of 1.8, nearly twice as volatile as Onyx. The price decline in this situation was probably more related to the weakness in the Technology sector and the market as a whole. But the 1.8 beta should have given some cautionary warning of lack of stability. (Beta is a measure of volatility. A beta of 1 is equal to the market in volatility. A beta of 2 is twice as volatile.)

## F I G U R E   2–2

Texas Instruments, Inc., January 1999–May 2003

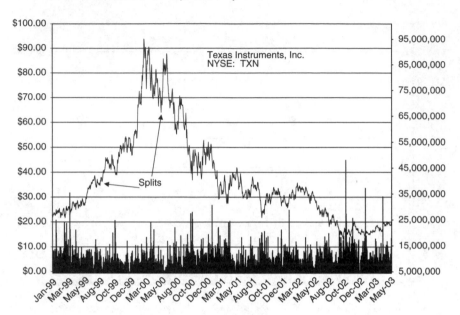

## OTHER FACTORS

Whether or not a share price will double is dependent on factors other than the current price. Again, it is earnings, or earnings growth potential, that investors are anticipating. They are all trying to buy the stock ahead of the earnings growth. The risk is always whether the earnings growth will in fact occur.

Many times the stock whose price is likely to double soon is the one whose price most recently doubled. This also has little if anything to do with the current market price. One might even say, forget the price and look at growth, growth potential, and anticipation. As dramatic evidence that the price level is unrelated to doubling, take a look at the highest-priced stock in the market, Berkshire Hathaway, Warren Buffett's incredible company.

The Berkshire Hathaway 10-year chart (Figure 2-3) shows the dramatic increases of the mid-1990s. The stock price had substantial gains, and it held on to most of them through the bear market. After the correction in February 2000, the price quickly retraced and achieved new highs.

**F I G U R E  2–3**

Berkshire Hathaway A, 1994-2004

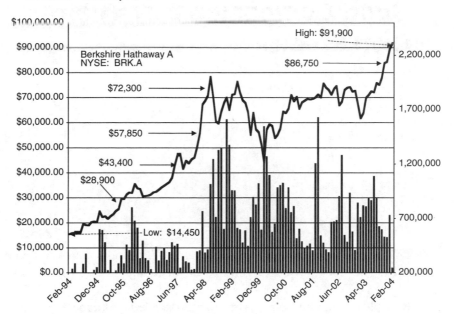

During the years 1994–1998, the stock was a four-bagger, increasing the original amount by four times. For the full 10 years it was a five-bagger, and nearly six.

When that stock price started at $14,450 per share, it was an incredible dollar increase for it to climb to $91,900 a share.

The important point to remember is that it's not the current price level alone that determines whether a stock will double in price. Rather, it's those factors that make the stock attractive to buyers.

# CHAPTER 3

# Good Companies Buy Their Own Stock

"**X**YZ Company has announced a purchase of 2 million shares of their own stock. The stock must be a good buy if the company itself is willing to buy."

It's still a common belief. The stockbroker tells a client, the client tells a friend, and so on, until a stock price begins to move upward. Many of these and other investors who heard the good news rush out to purchase more of the stock. The price continues to rise for the next few days and weeks. But is it really a good sign when a company announces a stock buyback?

Actually, company stock buybacks are often a mixed bag, with some good and some not so good effects. The Standard & Poor's 500 stocks in Table 3-1 announced stock buybacks in 2002.

In his 1999 Berkshire Hathaway annual report, Warren Buffett had this to say about stock buybacks:

> There is only one combination of facts that makes it advisable for a company to repurchase its shares: First, the company has available funds—cash plus sensible borrowing capacity—beyond the near-term needs of the business, and, second, finds its intrinsic value, conservatively calculated.

## WHY BUY THEIR OWN SHARES?

Companies have different motives for buying back their own shares. When employees exercise options, for example, earnings per share can quickly become diluted as the number of a company's shares outstanding grows.

## TABLE 3-1

Stock Buyback Announcements

| Company | Symbol | Date | No. Shares (Millions) | Price Then* | Price Now (2004) | % Change |
|---|---|---|---|---|---|---|
| Aflac | AFL | Feb. 12 | 25 | $24.55 | $35.00 | 42.0 |
| BB and T | BBT | Feb. 27 | 40 | 34.49 | 37.15 | 0.003 |
| Biomet | BMET | Mar. 26 | 30 | 26.12 | 38.98 | 48.0 |
| Bear Stearns | BSC | Jan. 8 | 20 | 56.69 | 87.84 | 45.0 |
| Health Mgt. Assoc. | HMA | Feb. 21 | 5 | 18.66 | 22.29 | 19.0 |
| Johnson & Johnson | JNJ | Feb. 13 | 80 | 56.04 | 53.91 | −8.0 |
| Lehman Brothers | LEH | Jan. 25 | 78 | 56.34 | 86.71 | 23.0 |
| Lexmark | LXK | Feb. 21 | 4 | 51.50 | 82.29 | 60.0 |
| MGIC Invest. Co. | MTG | Jan. 24 | 5.5 | 63.78 | 66.18 | 0.3 |
| Royal Dutch Petrol. | RD | Feb. 7 | 1.5 | 46.72 | 49.59 | 0.09 |
| Tenet Healthcare | THC | Feb. 14 | 10 | 41.37 | 2.02 | −71.0 |

*Adjusted for dividends and splits.

> That worry prompted Yahoo's move. Sometimes a buyback is a sign that a company is very bullish about its own prospects. And with Nasdaq stocks down, on average, over 40 percent since last summer, companies can buy a lot more shares for fewer dollars, potentially giving a bigger boost to earnings per share.[1]

Obviously, stock buybacks create more value in the stock, thereby giving something to the shareholder: value instead of a taxable dividend. Another obvious point is the positive image a company puts out by announcing a stock buyback. They wouldn't buy it if it were too expensive. Right?

## GOOD NEWS AND BAD NEWS

Companies also use buybacks when they have bad news to report. Obviously, the well-timed positive announcements are intended to soften the blow. It's the "we've got good news and bad news" situation. "We're going to buy back 8 percent of our stock … and, oh, by the way, our earnings are down 3 percent." The company is hopeful that the good news will outweigh the bad, and therefore the price impact will be neutral to positive.

---

[1] BusinessWeek, *"Taking Stock of Themselves,"* by Debra Sparks in New York, May 21, 2001

## T A B L E 3-2

Stock Buybacks*

| Date | Symbol | Company | Est. Buyback | Price Then | Price 4 months Later |
|---|---|---|---|---|---|
| 11/12/03 | MGG | MGM MIRAGE | 10M shares | $35.02 | $42.76 |
| 11/11/03 | BEV | Beverly Enterprises | $20M | 7.25 | 7.69 |
| 11/10/03 | MMM | 3M | Up to $1.5B | 78.84 | 84.77 |
| 10/29/03 | ODP | Office Depot | $50M | 15.17 | 16.96 |
| 10/15/03 | FCX | Freeport-McMoRan Copper & Gold | 20M shares | 37.19 | 29.65 |
| 10/9/03 | WTW | Weight Watchers | $250 | 38.49 | 38.79 |

*Source: RealTimeTraders.com

The good news/bad news technique is often used, even by some of the larger corporations. It can be quite effective.

As can be seen in Table 3-2, it's not just small companies—mega-corporations like 3M, MGM Mirage, and Beverly Enterprises are buying back shares. The price of 3M Company rose to $85.25 a share by the end of the year.

## DOES IT SHOW CONFIDENCE?

Sometimes companies will boldly announce their buyback intention with the statement that the stock has investment value at the current price. But considering the price impact of all that good publicity, one wonders. Is the announcement just more window dressing, or is the company sincere?

Short-term speculators have a great time with stock buyback announcements. To have a price rise several percentage points in just a few days is one of their dream selections. In fact, this is good for the spec-ulators in the short term but not necessarily helpful to investors in the long term. So what's the problem? Are companies dumb enough to pay prices that are actually too high? Peter Russ seems to think so. The following comments on stock buybacks are from *U.S. News & World Report:*

> The hitch. What could be wrong with this picture?
> Simply this: Many companies' shares are selling at or near record prices and may not be worth buying by anyone.
> Many analysts calculate a company's intrinsic value based on business potential rather than on the actions of excited buyers. When companies buy

their own shares at or below the "intrinsic value," they effectively create added value for the other shareholders. When they buy significantly higher than intrinsic value, they push the price up temporarily, but the value has to catch up in support. Paying that high price can cause problems.

"But the minute that you start paying a premium to buy back your stock," says Russ, "you are probably destroying value—using company money in a way that's not going to earn a great rate of return."[2]

## SHOULD WE BE WARY TODAY?

It's always good to be wary about the stock market. Historically, companies with too much money would either expand or return some money to shareholders in the form of dividends. The problem with dividends is that they are taxed. In fact, they are taxed twice, first as corporate income and second as investor dividends. Therefore, dividends aren't as popular as they once were.

Companies still like to show growth. They like to announce the opening of 200 additional retail outlets or the opening of a new plant to employ 2,000 workers. It's the kind of publicity that creates a warm feeling in the company's investors and customers. But what does it mean when the company is not expanding and is buying back its own shares? Don't they have anything better to do with the money? Have they run out of ideas? If they really think the company is undervalued, shouldn't they be investing the money in preparation for the new growth? These are real concerns the long-term shareholder and potential stock buyer should have.

Stock buybacks don't necessarily add significant value to a company's stock. The P/E ratios are too high and companies have too much cash, the cash being the reason they're willing to overpay. There's less risk in buying back their own shares than in new corporate growth, or at least less risk in how the actions are perceived by investors.

## ONLY AN ANNOUNCEMENT

Some stock buyback announcements are just that—announcements. Following the announcement, either the buyback never occurs or fewer shares are repurchased. Possibly the company originally intended to repurchase the shares, but things change and they are later unable to do so because the economics have changed. The financing became unavailable.

---

[2] Stephen Russ, quoted in Steven D. Kaye, "A Buyback Binge," *U.S. News & World Report*, February 17, 1997.

Although companies are occasionally accused of trumpeting a stock buyback for the purpose of supporting or accelerating the price, in reality that practice is unusual. The large majority of stock buyback activities are sincere.

## WHAT HAPPENS TO THE STOCK?

Much of the stock is effectively retired, clearing up some of the dilution problems. Other shares are used for employee retirement and stock option plans. Obviously, this is a good effect if the shares have true value, but a negative effect if they are overpriced.

Stock buyback announcements have many implications. In some cases it is a positive move for the company and its shareholders, even if only temporary. It improves the earnings per share since there are often fewer shares outstanding. And a stock price will often rise after a buyback announcement, especially in a rising market. However, the price can weaken and fall if negative news follows. An understanding of the company's announcement and the current true value of the stock can help an investor decide whether to buy or sell the stock.

# CHAPTER 4

# Heavy Volume, the Price Rises—Light Volume, the Price Falls

On the surface, this seems to make sense. When more investors become interested in a stock, they buy. The volume increases. Less interest means lower volume. Although this is true in some situations, it is not always evident. Whether or not this is true depends on several factors, including the current market strength and direction, as well as the strength and direction of an individual stock price.

To understand how volume may increase before prices increase, it is important to remember the existence of *limit sell orders*. Many times volume will suddenly increase; the price starts to increase and then falls slightly. Part of the reason for the decline is the presence of limit sell orders, or overhead supply. Another possible reason is nervous stock traders who buy on the volume increase but don't see the quick price advance and so bail out.

## Exxon Mobil

Exxon Mobil, a well-known oil company, has had the industry's share of difficulties with low oil prices. Because it is a commodity, the supply of oil needs to be controlled in order to keep prices high. If too much is produced, the market becomes competitive and prices fall, which has a negative impact on prices.

Looking at the price and volume chart for Exxon in Figure 4-1, you can pinpoint occasions when increased volume precedes an increase in the share

## FIGURE 4–1

Prices and Volume, Exxon Mobil Corporation, April 2001–January 2004

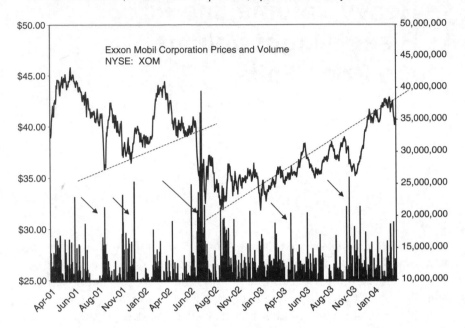

price (the five arrows). The volume increase in June 2002 is especially pronounced.

## ON-BALANCE VOLUME

Individual one-day spikes can also be significant signals, but notice that many of them are increased volume on a dropping price. Because of this, the signals can become confusing. Some investors counteract the confusion by using *on-balance volume* (OBV), by which they compare the volume to the price.

Developed by Joseph Granville, OBV can be a helpful indicator. It creates a volume line along the bottom of a price chart and is easily constructed. Start with a number that is relatively high, such as 50,000. On the first day, if the close is positive, that day's volume is added to the 50,000 beginning number. If the day's close ends lower, subtract the volume. On up days, add the volume, and on down days, subtract the volume. The result creates a fluctuating line.

On-balance volume can show an approaching trend change. The belief is that "smart money" sells a security when it's near a top, and smart money buys near a low. When the other investors catch on to a stock's rise in price, volume will increase and the OBV line will increase rapidly and faster. On the other side, on-balance volume will start to decrease while the price is still rising, indicating that the smart money is leaving the stock.

The on-balance volume is also informative when it is decreasing while the price is increasing (diverging). A signal is generated that the rally may not be strong. When the price is declining and the OBV is increasing, the investor shouldn't become too bearish, because a reversal could be coming.

## General Motors

Take a look at Figure 4-2 to see General Motors with its volume. In spring of 2002, there was a clear divergence as volume started a distinct decline while the price was rising. The price peaked at $68.00 and headed down finally to reach support at $41.32 in May. The volume increased as the stock fell to $31.00 a share in October. The volume continued to increase and the price began to rise. It corrected again to $30.00 in 2003 and kept the volume strong. Buyers came on the scene as the price began a slow climb.

## FIGURE 4–2

General Motors, January 2002–April 2004

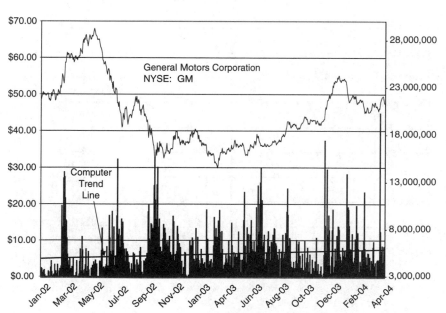

## MARKET VOLUME

Volume as an indicator for individual stocks can be informative or mis-
leading. However, volume as an indicator of the overall market can be significant. In general, the higher the volume, the greater the strength of the
market move.

When there is a 100-point move on the Dow Industrial Average, the
New York Stock Exchange volume will normally spike to a higher than
normal level. But it's not usually a spike that sends the signal; rather, it is
a broader change. If the NYSE volume has been averaging 500 million
shares a day but then steadily increases to 600 or 700 million shares a day,
the market also moves. When the Dow Industrials move 100 points on the
average or below the average volume, it is a sign of weakness. A market
move on weaker volume indicates that many large investors are skeptical,
which means that the likelihood of a reversal is high.

Take a look at the New York Stock Exchange volume chart in
Figure 4-3 for January 1997 through December 1998. Although it's
interesting to see the weakness before the October 1997 correction (the
Dow Industrials dropped more than 554 points), much of the rest of the
volume indicates strength. Volume surges are unlikely when they are

## FIGURE   4–3

Daily Volume, New York Stock Exchange, 1997–1998

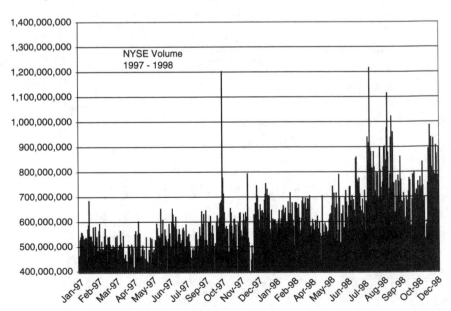

already near record levels. There is a weakness during the last half of December 1997, but that is not unusual for December, when many traders are on vacation.

Volume in 1998 jumped above the 600 million share mark and stayed there during January. It's interesting to note that this time period contains several record volume days for the New York Stock Exchange, as shown in Table 4-1.

The tallest single spike on the chart shows the day after (October 28) the big correction in the Dow Industrial Average. October 19 had the second largest volume, with the following day having the third largest volume for that period. These one-day volume records were accurate for the time of the chart. The strength coming back to the market after the October 1997 correction makes one wonder why the market corrected so sharply.

## T A B L E 4-1

NYSE Volume, October 28, 1997–
January 28, 1998*

| Daily Volume Records | Date |
|---|---|
| 1,201,347,000 | Oct. 28, 1997 |
| 791,946,000 | Dec. 12, 1997 |
| 776,331,000 | Oct. 29, 1997 |
| 754,111,000 | Jan. 29, 1998 |
| 745,003,000 | Jan. 9, 1998 |
| 711,969,000 | Oct. 10, 1997 |
| 710,903,000 | Jan. 28, 1998 |
| 2,812,919,000 | Jul. 24, 2002 |
| 2,673,242,000 | Jul. 19, 2002 |
| 2,623,758,000 | Jun. 28, 2002 |
| 2,578,284,000 | Jun. 25, 2002 |
| 2,442,421,000 | Jul. 23, 2002 |
| 2,367,955,000 | Sep. 17, 2001 |
| 2,316,879,000 | Sep. 21, 2001 |
| 2,268,402,000 | Jul. 22, 2002 |
| 2,149,946,000 | Sep. 19, 2001 |
| 2,137,653,000 | Jul. 11, 2002 |

*Source: NYSE Data Library.

# CHANGES IN VOLUME

Always look for changes in volume for clues to strength. Short-term and long-term changes both indicate strength, but the longer-term change is normally the most meaningful. In the short term, if the market rallies on weaker volume, the rally will not likely be sustained. If the market falls on light volume, it usually turns up fairly soon. Over the longer term, if the volume goes flat and then trends downward, it will often lead to a weaker market. The greatest strength is shown by an uptrend in the market index (Dow Industrial Average or Standard & Poor's 500 Index) and an uptrend in the volume. When these diverge, it often signals a change in direction.

# CHAPTER 5

# Watch the Bellwethers

*Bellwether* 1. A wether, or male sheep, which leads the flock, with a bell on its neck. 2. A leader of a thoughtless crowd.

*Webster's Collegiate Dictionary, 1960 edition*

Merriam-Webster possibly had the stock market in mind when adding the second definition of *bellwether*. (More recent editions of the dictionary have redefined a *bellwether* as "one that takes the lead or initiative" or as "an indicator of trends.") Stock market bellwethers are individual company stocks that are believed to lead the market. If a turn in the market is coming, those who watch these stocks believe the bellwether will turn first.

## INDUSTRY BELLWETHERS

Bellwethers can relate to the entire market, to a sector, or to an industry group. They might be leaders in Internet stocks or technology stocks. Someday you might read an article like the following:

> Technology stocks stabilized after Tuesday's slide on growing worries about slack demand in the computer industry. The technology-laden Nasdaq composite index, which tumbled nearly 25 points on Tuesday, fell 3.81 to 1,179.27, but several computer-industry bellwethers rebounded. Intel rose 1 to 71⅜ and Cisco Systems rose ½ to 53⅜.

The above quote lists Intel and Cisco Systems as bellwethers for the computer industry. When the term *bellwether* is used in this way, it is with a loose interpretation. More than a stock price that turns before the others, it is a descriptive term synonymous with *sector, industry,* or *market leader.*

If we look at the charts of Cisco Systems and Intel as compared to the Nasdaq Computer Index, we easily see that the prices of the two stocks track the index (Figures 5-1 and 5-2). Only on a few minor occasions does either price turn before the index. When a stock price follows an index closely, it is enough to consider it a bellwether, but it is obviously even better if the stock price turns before the index. One notable bellwether turn appears on the Intel chart in January 2004, when the price of Intel turned down before the Nasdaq Index.

## BIG BLUE

For many years the computer industry bellwether was the giant "Big Blue," that is, IBM. In fact, IBM is still considered a bellwether by many, not only for the computer industry, but also for the entire stock market. But since IBM ran into the realities created by the business use of personal

**F I G U R E   5–1**

Index Tracking, Intel Corporation, January 2003–April 2004

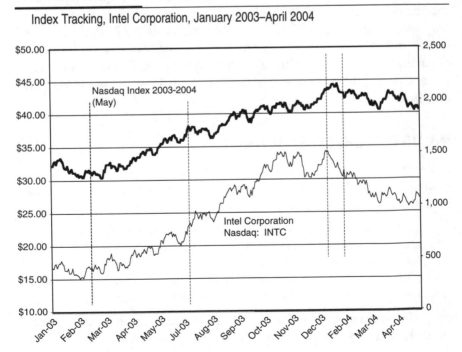

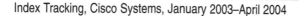

# FIGURE 5–2

Index Tracking, Cisco Systems, January 2003–April 2004

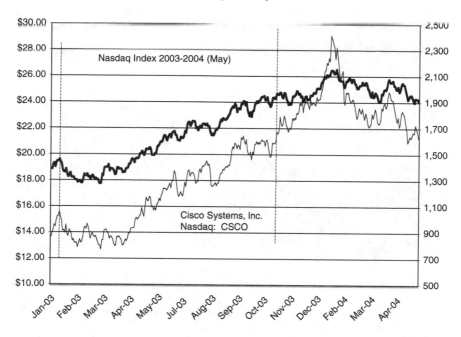

computers, its bellwether quality changed in the mind of many investors. During the first half of 1998, for instance, it looked as though IBM wasn't even part of the stock market (Figure 5-3).

## SOMETIMES YES, SOMETIMES NO

IBM tends to closely track the Dow Industrial Average. Although there are two obvious divergences in 2003 where IBM wandered off by itself (circled areas). A conclusion that can be drawn from Figure 5-3 is that sometimes IBM tracks the Dow Industrials closely and sometimes it does not. It is a bellwether in the sense of being a strong market participant—strong enough to be watched closely for market changes—but it is not a reliable forecaster of turning points. Even if it had such a tendency, it would probably not last long because stock traders would base trades on the direction of IBM, and it would therefore no longer behave as a bellwether.

The two circled areas clearly show that there are times when Big Blue's price can wander off by itself, with the rest of the market going its own way. Such actions raise much skepticism in the minds of bellwether skeptics. At point A in Figure 5-3, the Dow Industrial Average is clearly

## F I G U R E   5–3

IBM and Dow Industrial Average

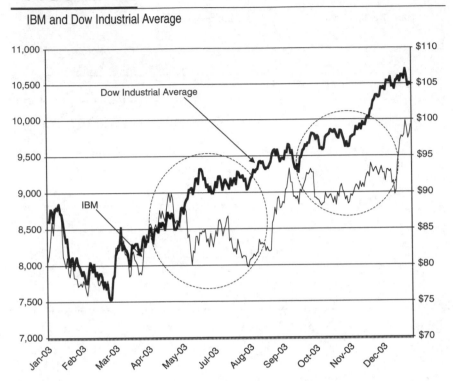

advancing while the price of IBM turns south. At point B the stock price suddenly advances as if trying to catch up with the average. A similar event occurs at point C. Finally, at point D both the Industrials and IBM retreat in an orderly fashion.

## THE PROBLEM OF SOPHISTICATION

Many wheeling-dealing stockbrokers and portfolio managers actively watch bellwethers. Their computer screens constantly display the stock quotes, blinking with each trade and changing color with each uptick or downtick in price. They believe the bellwether stocks give them one more indicator of the strength and direction of the stock market. If the market turns, they look to the bellwether for confirmation. A fair argument is that analysis of the stock market has become so sophisticated that the difference between bellwethers and the market indexes is negligible. One might not be able to use them as leaders, but rather, as confirming indicators.

It's not as easy for the individual investor to take advantage of bell-wethers. Although some stocks appear to be ahead of the market, the market doesn't wait long before making the change. An investor can't wait for an hour or two to decide whether the market will follow a change in the bellwether. Change tends to happen quickly.

# PART II

# Analysis

There are multitudinous ways to analyze companies and their common stock, but only one thing is important to the investor: an increase in price that is higher and faster than secure fixed income investments. This might relate to how well the business operates, but it's not always the case. There are poorly run businesses whose common stock is quite successful. Some of the successes in the airline industry illustrate this fact. The converse is also true: Some well-run businesses are terrible stocks. The company or its product line might be too small to be interesting to the stock market. This is why finance professors frequently do poorly when investing. They can find good companies, but the stock market doesn't like them.

Some knowledge of trends, both of the stock market and individual stocks, is important. Is the current market trend up, down, or in a secondary movement? How is the price trend of the individual stock related to the market trend?

In relation to trends, some knowledge of support and resistance can quickly tell the investor what is likely to happen in a sudden current movement. Looking back at three-year, five-year, and sometimes even 10-year price trends can give some excellent training in finding support and resistance levels.

# CHAPTER 6

# It's Always a Bull Market

In the longest of long runs, of course it's always a bull market. If it weren't, there wouldn't be anyone buying stock. It doesn't matter if you go back five, 10, 20 years, or more. You can look at the Dow Industrials, Standard & Poor's 500 Index, or the Nasdaq Composite. From all these charts, a similar bullish acceleration curve will appear (Figure 6-1).

As long as the stock market—any stock market—remains "fair and orderly," with an essentially free trading system and an economy that continues to grow, the market will follow.

However, although it's always a long-term bull market, some of the short-term damage can be severe. And it is not always a bull market for every publicly traded company. Sometimes companies that have been leaders in the past lose their ability to compete in an ever-changing marketplace. Other companies are poorly managed, and some never have much of a chance; therefore, selection is important and often difficult, but is the essence of prudent investing. As the renowned Peter Lynch once stated: "People should at least spend as much time selecting a stock as they do when buying a new refrigerator."

Investing for long-term growth is always less risky than trying to make a fortune in the next couple of weeks. Especially when an investor is just starting out, it is important to choose stocks on the conservative side. Leave the speculation to those who can afford it or have experience

**F I G U R E   6–1**

Always a Bull Market, Dow Industrial Average, 1998–2004

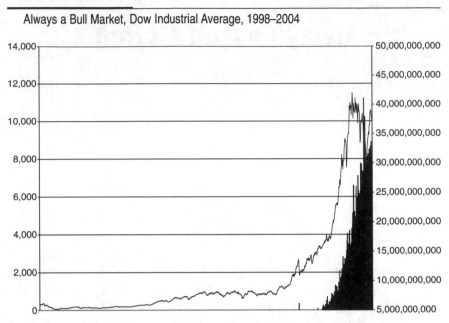

losing. An approach such as this will save you money and keep you interested in the stock market, which is still the most consistent money-mak-
ing investment in existence.

# CHAPTER 7

# Look for Divergence in Trends

The stock market seldom has a "normal day." Upon close analysis, each day is unique, with its own special pattern of change. One day, technology stocks will be hot and oil stocks will be out of favor. The next session might see oil stocks as the biggest gainers. One day the Dow Industrial Average will be up 60 points and the outlook for business development will appear favorable. The following session has the market correcting 100 points on the Dow, with growing inflation becoming a real threat.

## MARKET PREDICTIONS

As J. Pierpont Morgan so succinctly put it, the market will indeed "fluctuate"; it tends to do that during every trading session. When stockbrokers are asked the question, "What will the market do?" they will either attempt to be positive or neutral on the subject. Many analysts will give a lengthy explanation of what the market should do and why. But it's a simple fact that no one knows precisely what the overall stock market will do. The best one can hope for is to find a few signals of strength or weakness. One way to look for these signals is to look at trends.

## STOCK MARKET TRENDS

The concept of looking at stock market trends began in the late 1800s with Charles Henry Dow, one of the founding fathers of Dow Jones &

Company and the *Wall Street Journal.* Dow followed market trends based on the Dow Industrial Average and the Dow Railroad Average (now the Transportation Average). He followed what he called "primary, secondary, and tertiary" trends. The creation of the Dow averages and definition of trends formed the basis of the technical analysis used today. The study done by Dow and later by editor William Hamilton eventually became known as the "Dow theory." Here, we will look at trends in relationship to divergence, support, and resistance.

## Three Trends

The daily movements of the stock market, the *tertiary trends,* are important in the way they affect the secondary and long-term trends. The long-term trend, or *primary trend*, shows the overall direction of the stock market for an extended period of time, usually six months or more. The term *current trend* can refer either to the long-term trend or secondary trend, which is a short-term trend showing a reaction or move in the opposite direction to the primary trend.

## Stock Prices Move as a Group

One concept that all analysts agree on is that stock prices tend to move as a group. Dow Average, Standard & Poor's, and Nasdaq (over-the-counter) stocks tend to move as a group. If they diverge from moving as a group, it is a signal of weakness in the stock market.

The tendency of stock prices moving as a group is what makes up a trend. *Divergences* are changes in trend that show stocks not moving as a group. It is difficult to know whether the signal means a change in trend or the appearance of a secondary trend. However, the divergence is a technical signal of market weakness. There are also times when divergence occurs and the stock market ignores a divergence signal and continues to move upward. The investor who is aware of trends has the advantage of knowing whether the market is strong and in what direction it is going. First the divergence signal, then the reaction, followed by a turn in direction.

The sequence can be illustrated by the events surrounding the October 1987 crash:

- An all-time high for the Dow Industrials was reached in August.
- The Dow Utility Average had been declining since April.
- The Federal discount rate was raised, signaling a rise in interest rates.

- The reaction: The Dow Industrials drifted lower, down 200 points by October 19.
- Finally came the turn in the trend, as the Dow Industrial Average fell 508 points.

## SIGNALS

Signals can be confusing; a market trend can ignore what is supposed to happen and continue on its merry way. It is able to do this because it is a market of individuals making judgment calls.

Often, active investors wait for someone else to make a move. Groups form, believing the market will fall. Other groups form and take actions to prove the first group wrong. As the struggle ensues, buying or selling groups will gather and lose supporters until finally a majority of buyers or sellers emerges. The participants in this struggle will search out news and information to support their belief. If the news suggests their stand is incorrect, they will switch sides, and the market will move accordingly.

All the individual investor has to do is look for signals of a struggle or weakness. Such signals will often appear in trend divergence. It can be a divergence between the Dow Industrial Average and the Transportation Average, or it might be a divergence between the Dow and an individual stock.

### The October 1997 Divergence

On Monday, October 27, 1997, the Dow Industrial Average fell 554.26 points—a new record one-day drop for the prestigious Dow (although not a record percentage one-day decline). Although some analysts believed it was doomsday, others believed the drop to be a short-term correction. There was divergence between the Dow Industrial and Transportation Averages during the few weeks before the record correction.

When the Dow Industrial Average is compared to the Transportation Average, it's usually the transports that show weakness in relation to the industrials. In Figure 7-1 we see a strong uptrend in the transports, while the Industrial Average is declining. Also, the increased volatility, with the market surging back and forth, was a signal of weakness.

### NYSE Volume

A look at total NYSE volume for 1997 shows a cycling pattern, but not much in the way of a weakness signal. Although volume weakness appears

## FIGURE 7–1

Divergence of Dow Averages, August–December 1997

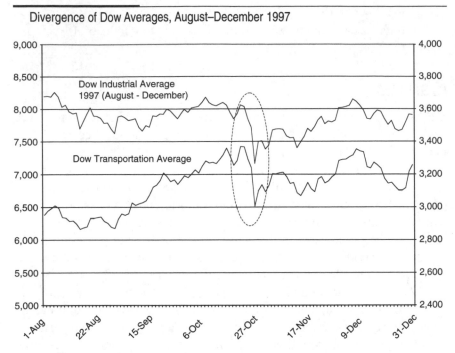

near the end of August and again near the end of September, it seems to be similar to earlier weakness events that did not cause such significant corrections.

The highest volume spike was actually the day after the big crash: 1,201,346,607 shares changed hands on October 28, 1997, another new record for one day of trading. The Dow Industrials regained more than 337 points, with the Transportation Average moving up better than 95 points. The strength was there; it was just time to test the market.

## What to Look For

Look at the relationship between the Dow Industrials, Dow Transportation Average, and, to some extent, the Dow Utility Average. If they are closely matching each other in direction and the volume is steady or growing, the market is strong. If the averages do not match direction or the volume is showing signs of weakness, the market is weak and could correct.

## Secondary Opportunities

When corrections are short-term secondary trends, they present buying opportunities to the investor. If the Dow Industrials drops more than 20 percent or is down for more than two consecutive months, it is considered the formation of a bear market. The investor might want to wait for signs of stabilization as shown by less volatility and trend confirmation.

# CHAPTER 8

# A Trend Remains in Force Until It Changes

**A** *trend* is a line drawn on a graph by connecting the points representing the closing price levels of a stock or point levels of an average or index. Trends of the stock market and of individual prices are an important part of investment analysis. Technical analysts and stock traders follow trends religiously. Even fundamental analysts keep an eye on trends for the same idea of strength and direction.

## CHARLES DOW

More than 100 years ago, Charles Henry Dow, founding father of Dow Jones and Company, as well as the *Wall Street Journal,* placed great importance on the study of trends and trend lines in the stock market. He compared stock market trends to the ocean tides washing up on the beach. By placing a stick in the sand, one can tell if the tides are coming in or going out. His analysis of the stock market was developed further by journal editor William Hamilton and was eventually called the *Dow Theory.* Some analysts still follow the theory or at least make use of some of its components.

### The Three Trends

Dow said there are three important types of trends in the stock market:

- Primary trends: The long-term trends of the market over months and years,

- Secondary trends: Short-term trends of a few days or weeks, running contrary to the long-term trend.

- Tertiary trends: The daily movements of the stock market.

Figure 8–1 shows the activity in the Dow Industrial Average from January 1999 to May 2004. During 1999 and 2000 the market was in a slow uptrend. In 2001 it corrected and fell into a downtrend Although the impact of 9/11 (2001) was a factor, notice that the market was already in a decline, which would become a secondary trend. It's entirely possible that this was the beginning of the bear market that followed, but the events of 9/11 caused large investors to attempt to give support to a threatened stock market. This caused a rally and the bear was delayed.

## The Strongest Trend

The strongest trend is the primary trend. The market can have expected or unexpected weakness where the Dow Industrial Average drops more than 500 points but recovers. In these situations, the primary trend remains strong.

## FIGURE 8–1

Trends, Dow Industrial Average, 1994–2004

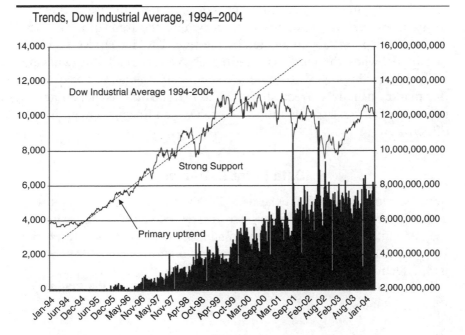

When an uptrend changes direction and breaks through the trend line, it is a signal of stock market weakness that could become a reversal. Breaking through the trend line is the key indicator. Sometimes the signals are false and the primary trend continues. Other times the trend turns. It all depends on what happens after the trend line has been crossed.

## WHERE TO DRAW THE LINES

When a person first begins drawing trend lines on a stock market chart, the question occurs as to where the lines should be drawn. The inadequate (although accurate) short answer is to "draw them where you want—they're your lines." Here are some more useful guidelines:

Uptrend: Draw the uptrend line underneath the data point lows.

Downtrend: Draw the trend line on top of the data point highs.

The main reason for these two locations is that they will clearly show where the trend changes direction and breaks through the line.

### A Best Fit Approach

There are many opinions as to where trend lines should be drawn. The ideal is to figure out where the professionals think the trend lines are located. Interestingly, this tends to be where the trend line fits best. Several data points are connected by the line. The line shows examples of support when the market is trading above the trend and resistance when it's trading below. If there are secondary trends, it's easy to see the market usually correct sharply if the trend line is penetrated. It takes practice and experimentation to see which line placement is most effective.

### Data Point Extremes

Some say to draw trend lines at data point extremes. This does not work well because doing so totally bypasses many secondary trends. Although the trend line will show some areas of support, it will not show resistance. Drawing lines at extreme ends of data may work for technical patterns, but isn't effective for reliable trend lines.

Figure 8-2 shows a well-defined primary uptrend in the Standard & Poor's 500 Index.

Standard & Poor's 500 Index, January 2002–March 2004

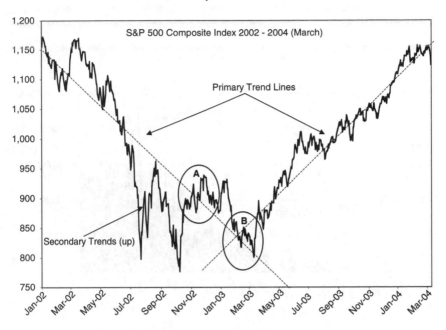

## Length of Time

Here again, the length of time a chart covers is up to the person making the charts. Twelve to 18 months are usually good for determining the primary trend. Once that is established, secondary trends are easy to see.

A longer period chart can be an interesting reference for the analyst to see where the current trend is coming from. If we look at the long-term chart from 1994 through 2004 in Figure 8-3, we see some interesting points: a good bull market uptrend from 1994 to 2000, with strong secondary action in 1996, 1997, and 1998.

## FINAL NOTES

Although plotting trends can help an investor understand the stock market, it is important to remember the factor of anticipation. The stock market constantly attempts to anticipate what will happen next. Anticipation is often unfulfilled or entirely incorrect. The trend remains in force until the trend changes. The difficulty is in knowing if the trend has changed or

## FIGURE 8–3

Standard & Poor's Index, 1994–2004.

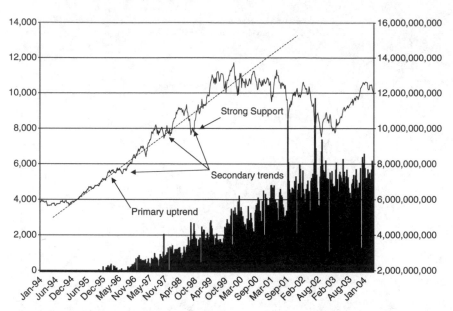

a correction is just a secondary trend. That's why the market tends to correct sharply if the uptrend line is penetrated. Also, like other stock market indicators, the importance of the trend can be overridden by other events.

It's easy to see the primary trend turn in February of 2003, and go into an extended uptrend. A weakness occurred in March 2004 that could become a larger concern. At the time the chart was made it was impossible to tell if it would be an actual turn in the primary trend or was just a secondary trend development.

# CHAPTER 9

# Look for Insider Trading

Insiders of a corporation are the decision makers and strategy formulators. They are the directors, the officers, and the high-level "line" personnel. If anyone knows what's going on in a company, it is the managers who are directly involved in the upper-level decision-making process.

## ILLEGAL VS. LEGAL

In a broad sense, it is illegal for anyone to buy or sell shares of stock in the United States based on information not yet available to the public. Examples of *insider trading* cases that have been brought by the SEC are cases against:

- Corporate officers, directors, and employees who traded the corporation's securities after learning of significant, confidential corporate developments
- Friends, business associates, family members, and other "tippees" of such officers, directors, and employees, who traded the securities after receiving such information
- Employees of law, banking, brokerage, and printing firms who were given such information to provide services to the corporation whose securities they traded
- Government employees who learned of such information because of their employment by the government

- Other persons who misappropriated, and took advantage of, confidential information from their employers

Because insider trading undermines investor confidence in the fairness and integrity of the securities markets, the SEC has treated the detection and prosecution of insider trading violations as one of its enforcement priorities.

The SEC adopted new Rules 10b5-1 and 10b5-2 to resolve two insider trading issues where the courts have disagreed. Rule 10b5-1 provides that a person trades on the basis of material nonpublic information if a trader is "aware" of the material nonpublic information when making the purchase or sale. The rule also sets forth several affirmative defenses or exceptions to liability. The rule permits persons to trade in certain specified circumstances where it is clear that the information they are aware of is not a factor in the decision to trade, such as pursuant to a preexisting plan, contract, or instruction that was made in good faith.

Rule 10b5-2 clarifies how the misappropriation theory applies to certain nonbusiness relationships. This rule provides that a person receiving confidential information under circumstances specified in the rule would owe a duty of trust or confidence and thus could be liable under the misappropriation theory.

For more information about insider trading, please read "Insider Trading—A U.S. Perspective," a speech by staff of the SEC (available at http://www.sec.gov/answers/insider.htm).[1]

The basic idea of insider trading is simple: If a person has important information that will influence the price of a company's shares, the law is broken if that person uses the information for buying or selling stock. It is also illegal for anyone trading on the information (or even on the act), even if they have no direct connection with the company. In other words, if a stockbroker observes a CEO of a company selling stock and also makes a similar transaction, the broker is guilty of insider trading.

## FAIR AND ORDERLY MARKET

Disallowing trades based on inside information is important. It is part of the *fair and orderly market* concept now being adhered to by all the world's stock exchanges. If such activities were allowed or ignored by the authorities, the public securities market would lack integrity, without which they could not function. Why trade stocks or other securities if others have a distinct advantage? Stock market prices are driven by anticipa-

---

[1] http://www.sec.gov/answers/insider.htm

tion based on information. Making trades based on privileged information, ahead of the public, amounts to fraud. Individual investors need to have the same information as the professional investors in order for the public markets to be a level playing field for all.

## INSIDERS MUST REPORT

At times corporate employees are privy to inside information, and they want to legitimately buy and sell their company's stock. For various reasons, such information cannot be immediately released to the public. In fairness, the insiders are allowed to trade, but they must report transactions, holdings, and other information. A sense of fairness is maintained because the public is able to view and assess such transactions.

### SEC Insider Forms

According to the Securities Exchange Act of 1934, an insider is defined as an officer or director of a public company, or an individual or entity owning 10 percent or more of any class of a company's shares. The definition in all its legal speak is given in Section 16 of the 1934 act; there are further words sparred on how more specifically to define an "officer" and "beneficial owner" in Rule 16a-1 of the Code of Federal Regulations.

For all the legal definitions of *titles* and *share owners*, what the rule says is that anyone involved in the inner workings of a publicly traded company is an insider. The concern is that this person could gain an unfair advantage over the rest of the public when trading company shares. Therefore, an insider must register by making a statement of holdings (SEC Form 3) within 10 days. Changes in ownership must be filed by the tenth day of the month following the transaction (SEC Form 4).

At the end of the fiscal year, an insider or former insider must file Form 5 within 45 days. Its intent is to prevent people from moving in and out of insider status. Obviously, Form 4 gives the most useful information to investors. It answers the question of what the insiders are doing, whether buying or selling, as well as their current holdings in the company. Information on insider trades, available on the Internet and through several newsletters, is usually based on this SEC form.

### Form 144 Stock

Form 144, used by the SEC to track insider information, is for those currently holding securities that are not registered. The form is the last step, allowing the shares to be sold on the open market and be publicly traded. It allows the shares to be sold but ensures that the number is relatively small and that the seller isn't an underwriter bringing a new issue to market.

The form tells how many shares will be sold within the following three months. If they are not sold, the form must be amended. In the real world, by the time the investor sees the Form 144 information, the shares have been sold. Many will file the 144 and Form 4 at the same time.

## SIGNIFICANT TRADES

Those who follow insider transactions claim that buys are usually more significant than sells. Some people also argue that corporate insiders tend to avoid making transactions because they know the public is watching. Instead, they rely on their stock option benefit to supply them with company shares. Another side to this suggests that an insider or group of insiders could influence the share price by buying stock on the open market. These considerations are some of the reasons the value of watching insider transactions is often debated.

### Two Situations

#### Rise in Number of Insider Buys
Some people view an increase in the number of insider buys as an additional reason to buy a stock. They believe that a sudden flurry of insider buys is a positive statement of growth potential for the company. It is important to keep in mind, however, that sometimes companies lend money to their employees to buy stock, with the intention of having the public see the buys. Such corporate strategies suggest a manipulation of public interest; therefore it is important to view the presence of insider trades in relation to other information about a company.

#### Media Attention
If the insider's trading has been significant enough to be discussed in the financial news media, it calls additional attention to the activity. The extra attention from the news appearance can affect the stock's price. However, the impact follows right on the heels of the announcement. If an investor plans to take action based on the news, he or she must do so quickly. Waiting even a day or two can be too late.

## Part of the Picture

Obviously, an investor can follow insider trading as an investment strategy by itself. However, investment professionals recommend the use of additional analysis to form a conclusion before taking action. Corporate insiders can have any one of several reasons or motives for buying and selling their company's stock. Therefore, it is prudent to use information on insider trades as part of the picture of a company rather than as a sole indicator.

## Sells vs. Buys

Unless there are several insiders selling the same stock, sells are generally not meaningful as an indicator. Insiders are often selling stocks to raise cash to purchase items other than the company's stock. A new car, boat, or a down payment on a lake cabin can be motivators for the insider. Also important is the strength of the individual sector or the entire stock market. If a market sell-off is in progress, it would not be particularly meaningful to see company insiders selling stock also.

# WHAT'S THE MARKET DOING?

Yes, the insiders are selling. But should you?

The headline of a *New York Times* article poses the titular question. Heavy insider selling is usually thought to be a bearish signal. The *Times,* however, relies on work by Nejat Seyhun, a finance professor at the University of Michigan to suggest that the current wave of selling is not necessarily pro-bear.

> [Seyhun explains that] the new wave of insider selling has occurred while the stock market has been rallying. His research has found that such selling carries far less bearish significance than selling during a market decline.
>
> To document this difference, Professor Seyhun looked at each publicly traded company on the New York and American stock exchanges and the Nasdaq market from the beginning of 1975 to the end of 2000, identifying all months when the company's insiders were net sellers.
>
> Professor Seyhun found that when insiders sold during a decline, the stocks they sold lagged behind the overall market by an average of 5 percent over the next 12 months…. In contrast, Professor Seyhun found no discernible pattern in the subsequent performance of stocks sold by insiders while the market was rallying.

As a result, he concludes, the current high level of insider selling provides no signal for the market's direction. He advises investors who base their equity exposure on the behavior of insiders to "sit tight and watch both stock prices and insider trading" in the coming months.(See http://www.typepad.com/t/trackback/171992.)

# LOGICALLY, BUYS CAN HAVE MORE SIGNIFICANCE

Buys can have significance, although again, they should not be the only consideration for selecting a stock. Does it work? The answer is mixed, but one can find evidence of successful situations based on insider buys.

### First, the Obligatory Caution

Results can vary when the activities of others are used as a forecasting tool. What works on one occasion might be a dismal failure on the next. All stock market analysis systems are capable of sending false signals. The investor needs to be aware of this and not rely too heavily on any one system of analysis.

### Strong Positives

Standard & Poor's CompuStat, a market data provider, compiles numbers on insider stock activity. CompuStat tracks the buying and selling of shares by the top 10 individuals—based on the number of shares bought or sold—having an insider relationship with a company, using information gathered from Securities and Exchange documents.

Based on CompuStat data, we looked for companies where the transaction values of insider purchases over the last 12 months exceeded those of insider sales in the same period by a ratio of at least 10 to 1 (transaction values are derived from the number of shares bought or sold, multiplied by the prevailing purchase or sale price at the time). A ratio that high may be an indication of strong positive sentiment on the part of company insiders. The stocks had to pass one final test: Each had to carry a ranking of four stars (accumulate) or five stars (buy) from Standard & Poor's equity analysts. These rankings indicate that analysts expect the stocks to outperform the market over the next six to 12 months.

After we ran the numbers, 22 stocks emerged, which are listed in Table 9-1.

Which of these stocks do you wish you had bought back in April 2002? Well, it was a bear market, after all. The bear market clobbered

## T A B L E 9–1

Companies with Insider Trading, 2002–2004*

| Company | Apr 02 | Apr 03 | Mar 04 |
|---|---|---|---|
| Allegheny Energy (AYE) | $41.78 | $9.9 | $12.26 |
| Amphenol (APH) | 43.06 | 38.96 | 59.57 |
| Certegy (CEY) | 41.86 | 24.37 | 33.41 |
| Charter Communications (CHTR) | 9.41 | 1.08 | 4.42 |
| Ecolab (ECL) | 22.60 | `24.16 | 27.59 |
| Edison International (EIX) | 17.02 | 3.87 | 23.17 |
| El Paso Energy (EP) | 43.00 | 6.25 | 6.89 |
| John Hancock (JHF) | 39.95 | 28.36 | 40.99 |
| Hologic (HOLX) | 14.8 | 9.05 | 19.50 |
| Immunex (IMNX) | | (Bought out by Amgen) | |
| Keithley Instruments (KEI) | 20.21 | 11.36 | 19.40 |
| Kinder Morgan Ene Partners (KMP) | 33.16 | 38.24 | 45.24 |
| Kraft (KFT) | 40.00 | 28.37 | 32.47 |
| Liberty Media (L) | 26.70 | 18.55 | 11.53 |
| Midway Games (MWY) | 32.60 | 3.82 | 6.58 |
| Pactiv (PTV) | 20.34 | 19.89 | 21.71 |
| Phelps Dodge (PD) | 40.08 | 32.40 | 80.70 |
| Pre-Paid Legal (PPD) | 26.70 | 18.55 | 24.41 |
| Prudential Financial (PRU) | 32.60 | 29.97 | 44.84 |
| Sanmina-SCI (SANM) | 9.96 | 4.33 | 10.99 |
| Sovereign Bancorp (SOV) | 14.31 | 14.48 | 20.99 |
| Weingarten Realty (WRI) | 36.43 | 40.00 | 20.99 |

*De Guia is a portfolio services analyst for Standard & Poor's. (Any advice, analysis, or recommendations contained in articles labeled "Insight from Standard & Poor's" refloct the views of Standard & Poor's, which operates separately from and independently of BusinessWeek Online. It is possible that BWOL may from time to time publish information that is not consistent with advice, analysis, or recommendations that are published by Standard & Poor's. Standard & Poor's and BusinessWeek Online are each units of the McGraw-Hill Companies, Inc. BusinessWeek Online, April 2002.) [PBG19]

nearly every one of these selections. You might say that during a real bear, all bets are off. Very likely Immunex, Inc. being bought by Amgen was the brightest light in the bunch. Looking at the table makes you think that things could have been better if the bear had not come around, obviously.

It also makes you wonder if the insiders were buying because they had a fear of growing price weakness and an approaching down market. Also obvious, any attempts to give support to falling prices were exercises in futility.

So where does that leave us with insider trading?

There is logic to buying being most meaningful in a bull market, where other stocks are also attractive. However, if the market is becoming volatile or trending down, any buying might well be a poor attempt at gleaning price support from other investors. Insider selling is pretty much meaningless or illegal, depending on the circumstance.

# CHAPTER 10

# Know the Best Type of Order

There are many different types of stock orders an investor can place. Some are of debatable value and are seldom used. Following are simplified descriptions of some of the basic types of orders.

## MARKET ORDER

Best available price; it should be filled as soon as possible. For example, an investor calls a broker and learns that shares for XYZ Corp. are trading at 55.25 to 55.375 and the last trade was at 55.375. The investor says: "I want to place a market order to buy 200 shares of XYZ at the market." Computers make this order easy to enter and easy to fill. In all likelihood the investor can get a verbal confirmation of the order execution while still on the phone. The broker comes back to the phone and says: "Confirming a buy of 200 shares of XYZ at the market. The order was filled at 55.375. The settlement is *regular* way," which means the current trade date plus three days, or T + 3.

The main advantage of this type of order is that it's placed and filled immediately. The disadvantage is that it's impossible to know the price ahead of time.

## LIMIT ORDER

Specific acceptable price; it should be filled when the trade can be completed at the order price or better. If the order cannot be filled, it remains as a limit order until canceled. It can be entered as a one-day-only order or as a *good-till-canceled* (GTC) order. For example, "Buy 200 XYZ at a limit price of 55, good for today only." The order is entered by the broker. If 200 XYZ can be purchased at $55 a share or better, the order is executed. If the limit is not activated, the order is automatically canceled at the end of the trading session.

## BUY STOP ORDER

Best available price once the stop price is traded on or through. "Buy 200 XYZ with a buy stop at 59. Put the order in, Good till canceled." The buy stop is placed above the current trading price. The investor wants to buy the stock only if the price is moving up. The order to buy 200 shares will become a market order if XYZ stock trades at $59 a share or higher. If the order is not executed within a time specified by the brokerage firm—usually end of the month, 30 days, or the end of the following month—it is canceled.

## SELL STOP ORDER

Be careful with stop orders. If they are too close to the current price, the specialist will come after them. Some investors make the mistake of placing stop orders within 10 percent of the current price. Many times the end result of this strategy is to doom their investment portfolio to a 10 percent loss.

   The sell stop is placed below the current market price. The price should be selected by checking a chart of price movement. The sell stop is considered a defensive strategy, selling the stock in a sharp decline.

## STOP LIMIT ORDER

Specific acceptable price, once the stop price is traded on or through. The limit price can be placed at the same price as the stop or at an entirely different price from the stop price. If the order cannot be filled, it remains as a limit order until canceled.

   "Sell 200 shares of XYZ at a stop of 48, with a limit of 46, Good till canceled." The stop will be triggered if the price of XYZ Corp. trades at or through $48, and will sell immediately if—and only if—the order can be executed at $46 a share or better. Again, the unexecuted order will remain in the system for a length of time designated by the brokerage firm unless the order is canceled.

## MARKET IF TOUCHED

Market If Touched (MIT) is an order qualifier for buy orders placed below the current trading price and sell orders placed above the current price. It is executed if the security trades at or through the current price. Effectively, MITs are the opposite of stop orders in terms of dynamics. They are used extensively with futures trading.

## MARKET ON OPEN

Market on Open, or On the Open, is an order that specifies the market opening as an activator. This order does not guarantee the opening price. Obviously, it must be placed before the market opens.

## MARKET ON CLOSE

Market on Close, or On the Close, is an instruction to a stock exchange floor broker to execute the trade at the best available price during the last 30 seconds of the trading session. There are no guarantees that the order will be filled or that it will be filled at the final trading price.

# CHAPTER 11

# Institutions Show Where the Action Is Now

"Any stock in too many institutional portfolios or the subject of excess advisory bullishness should be suspect. Some day a majority will want to take profits."

GERALD M. LOEB

There are two considerations regarding institutional investing. First, can the small individual investor compete with the big money managers? And second, should individuals select or avoid stocks owned by large institutions?

## DAVID AND GOLIATH

Institutional investors are professional money managers for corporations, pension funds, mutual funds, and other investment companies. Their strategies may be long term or short term, and they implement these strategies by moving the market by buying and selling stock. Fund managers might do their own analysis or hire others to do the basic analysis for them. Every business day they deal with large amounts of money. Obviously, they have advantages not available to the individual investor. Possibly the biggest advantage to the institutional investor is the large amount of money available to them. Because of this, they can make larger trades, thereby profiting from small price moves, and they can afford to make more mistakes.

When it comes to analysis, the only real advantage held by the institutional investor is experience. According to securities laws, information is made available to the public at the same time. The only exceptions are corporate insiders who were involved in the decision-making process. However, they must report any transactions to the Securities and Exchange Commission.

Institutional stock traders are the professionals of the market. They are involved with stock trading on a constant basis, some would even say 24/7. Many of them not only remember what happened yesterday, but last week as well. These are important differences between them and the individual investor, who might have $10,000 or $100,000 to invest, and who sweats bullets to get it accomplished. The professional institutional investor might have $3 million or $500 million to invest in the next 15 minutes. When that's done, they take on the next challenge. They are usually not too worried about one or two stocks (unless they're heavily into WorldCom or Enron), but worry more about world economics for the next six months. More important, they worry more about how emotionally the stock market will react to news.

## THEY'RE NOT ALWAYS RIGHT

Institutional stock traders aren't always right. In fact, they are frequently wrong. Peter Lynch, the former renowned fund manager for Fidelity's Magellan Fund, refers to them as the "blundering herd."

Lynch knows much about institutional investors and the things they do to make money through investing. Professional, institutional investors now dominate the investing markets. He believes this fact often leads people to believe (incorrectly) that the individual has no chance in the stock market. In reality, amateur investors now have improved chances for success in the market if they do their homework and know their companies well.

As Lynch puts it:

> He or she can take an independent tact by zigging when the Herd zags and buying stocks that the Herd has overlooked, and especially the ones that the Herd has recently trampled. What holds them back is the inferiority complex they've gotten from mistaking the cattle drive for the Atlanta Braves.

This is reminiscent of stock trader Jessie Livermore's philosophy of winning big when you know you're right, as described in Chapter 20. The thundering herd analogy possibly refers to the earlier days of America, when cattle drives were used to deliver beef to market. Drovers would work hard to keep the herd calm and quiet. Large groups of cattle tend to excite easily and stampede mindlessly off in one direction, just as do investors in their panic selling.

### Not Like the Braves

Lynch likes the Atlanta Braves. As a professional baseball team, they know what they're doing, at least most of the time. It's the clueless cattle that represent the actions of institutional investors when the stock market goes crazy. Thanks to good public relations work, many individuals believe the professionals know what they're doing, all the time. The fact is, the professionals don't always know. They do make mistakes—big ones. The belief still exists, however, and, according to Lynch, causes many individual investors to develop that "inferiority complex."

The inferiority complex can cause investors to do three self-destructive things:

1. Imitate the professionals, buying "hot" stocks or trying to "catch the turn" in IBM or other stocks.
2. Become "sophisticated" and invest in futures, options, or options on futures.
3. Buy what they've heard has been recommended by a magazine or by one of the popular financial programs.

Information on what the pros think is so readily available that the celebrity tip has replaced the old-fashioned tip from Uncle Harry as the most compelling reason to invest in a company.

Catching the turn with IBM, or any stock, means going up against professionals who can be profitable for an eighth or can afford to take the loss if they miss. Futures, options, and so on, can be an even faster spin with which to lose money. As for stock tips, some are good, some are bad, but most are old, and the opinion could have changed more than once by the time the investor takes action. Such tips should never be the only reason for selecting a stock.

## THE INDIVIDUAL'S EDGE

Instead of becoming self-destructive, take advantage of special investing edges that individuals have. Two kinds of edges are too often overlooked by investors:

There's the "on-the-job edge," in which one has a working relationship with either an industry or the related companies with whom the investor conducts business. And there's the "consumer's edge," with which the individual investor can capitalize on his or her experiences in, for example, restaurants, airports, and shopping malls.

Thus, individuals can derive advantages from what they do for a living and for fun, such as shopping as a consumer. Investing in the stock of an employer or a competitor makes sense. Often, the competitor is the better selection, and there is less chance of being too forgiving if things don't turn out as expected.

As a first rough screen, going shopping can provide a whole list of possible investment opportunities. Which stores have great products and great service? Do they look as though they plan to be around for a while? Do the stores have several customers? Are the customers browsing or buying? These observations should be just the beginning.

Make a list of the best stores, then do the important background research. The research is extremely important, so that the investor doesn't just buy the glitzy presentation of a particular business. Select companies with good-looking fundamentals, a reasonable price, and a great-looking future. Buy the stock and watch the new developments.

Standard & Poor's came up with a list of nine companies whose stocks they expect to do well in 2004. The stocks were selected as Five Star, which is the S&P equity analyst rating for stocks expected to outperform the market in the next year. As well, they were selected by secure earnings and dividend histories. In Table 11-1, we also add the percent institutional ownership.

Whether the herd is thundering, stumbling, or just rumbling, it can be a distinct advantage to be in front of it, unlike the cattle herds of days long gone. Being ahead of the herd in the stock market can bring a lot of quick profit. Following the herd can be a different story. Pick the good quality stocks, the companies with good value that the herd is likely to stumble across in the next few months.

## HOW MUCH INSTITUTIONAL OWNERSHIP?

It is an oft-stated belief that 20 to 30 percent institutional ownership of a company's stock is an enviable situation. The institutions like it; therefore, it must be a good stock. Although a certain amount of institutional ownership of a stock can be an advantage, like the difficulties encountered by the sorcerer's apprentice, it is possible to have too much of a good thing.

## T A B L E   11-1

Institutional Ownership*

| Company(Ticker) | S&P Stars Rank | S&P Earn & Div. Rank | Institutional Ownership % |
|---|---|---|---|
| Anheuser-Busch (BUD) | 5 | A+ | 59.8 |
| Automatic Data Processing (ADP) | 5 | A+ | 69.6 |
| Capital One (COF) | 5 | A+ | 82.4 |
| Cardinal Health (CAH) | 5 | A+ | 77.5 |
| Citigroup (C) | 5 | A+ | 64.2 |
| Compass Bancshares (CBSS) | 5 | A+ | 34.9 |
| MBNA (KRB) | 5 | A+ | 77.0 |
| Omnicom Group (OMC) | 5 | A+ | 81.9 |
| Sysco (SYY) | 5 | A+ | 68.6 |

*Stock list appeared in *BusinessWeek Online*, January 9, 2004, in an article by Michael Kaye, CFA.

The problem lies in sudden sellouts and profit-taking. Stocks with large institutional ownership might have adequate shares for trading in normal, steady markets, but markets can change suddenly. If 50 or 70 percent of the stockholders are institutions and they begin selling, their quick exit can be devastating to the stock price.

### How Much Is Too Much?

To begin with, it's not as easy to find stocks without any institutional ownership. It's estimated that institutions own at least 50 percent of the entire stock market. So how much is enough, and what constitutes too much institutional ownership? If the problem caused by institutions is price volatility, perhaps *that* should become the issue rather than the amount of ownership.

## SELLING IN UP MARKETS

Selling of heavily institutionally owned stock could occur in a strong up market. Sometimes even a fundamentally sound company that has satisfactory earnings growth and is 50 to 60 percent owned by institutions can experience a sell-off in a market rally. If the stock is not participating in the rally and shows light volume, with few buyers or sellers, some institutions become nervous and start to sell. Financial markets are tightening their focus on the short term. If a stock is not matching the pace, they sell. Many believe there's too much focus on the short-term result.

Indeed, the U.S. economy and financial system suffer from "short-termism," an affliction caused by a lack of attention to long-term economic performance. Financial markets put pressure on corporate managers to focus too much on quarterly profits and too little on patient investment for the long haul.

The market continues to rally, but the nonparticipant just sits in the institution's portfolio. Eventually the institutional holders decide to sell the nonparticipant and buy a stock with more action. Sellers quickly outnumber buyers, and the stock price drops, even though the overall market is still advancing

## PERCENTAGE OWNERSHIP

Some analysts claim that the percentage of institutional ownership is not as important as the number of institutions owning the stock. If 100 or 200 institutions own 70 percent of one stock, a problem will arise if they all sell at the same time. Obviously, no one can argue with that logic.

However, there are three facts that somewhat offset the too-much-institutional-ownership debate:

1. Stocks with larger institutional ownership tend to be market leaders.
2. It is difficult to find a good stock that is not heavily owned by institutions.
3. If the institutions don't like the stock, significant price growth is unlikely.

## WHAT ABOUT THE INSTITUTIONS?

With institutional investors accounting for half of the market, avoiding them is nearly impossible. Even if it were possible to find a great stock before the herd thundered in, the price action would need the buying by institutions before it showed significant movement. For the value investor, institutional ownership should be a consideration, but it should not be the sole criterion on which to decide.

Many companies have done well even though they have always had a high level of institutional ownership. Microsoft is a good example. Even now, more than 35 percent of the shares are owned by institutions. AT&T

has 44.4 percent institutional ownership. General Electric has an institutional ownership of 49.9 percent. General Motors has 64.2 percent institutional ownership. It's a safe bet to say that few hesitate to own shares in any of these companies just because the institutional ownership is higher than average.

## THE SIGNIFICANCE OF INSTITUTIONAL OWNERSHIP

Rather than trying to figure out whether the amount of institutional ownership is too high or too low, learn why the institutions like or dislike a stock. Why do they like General Motors and General Electric? Why don't more of them like Apple Computer? This type of analysis will give the individual investor a better idea of what gets the professionals excited. Understanding this can help with the stock selection process.

# CHAPTER 12

# It Depends on Support and Resistance

**U**nderstanding the basic concept of support and resistance informs the investor of the significance of stock market moves. It can send a signal of strength or weakness in a specific move. It can tell the likelihood.

## THE DOW THEORY

The idea of market support and resistance goes back to the Dow theory, originated by Charles Dow and further developed by a later editor of the *Wall Street Journal*, William Hamilton.

*Support* is a point in a declining stock market where buyers start buying. *Resistance* is the point where sellers start selling. When a market declines, analysts look lower for the next area of support. The strength of an area of support is determined by how many times the level stopped former declines. If it stopped only once, it is weak support. If market declines stopped at the same level more than once, it is stronger support. When the market falls through strong support, it has a tendency to drop much further.

Resistance, the opposite of support, is a level where stock market advances stopped in the past, where stock buyers stopped buying. If advances were stopped only once or maybe twice, it is weak resistance. If several advances were stopped, it is stronger resistance. When the market breaks through resistance, it tends to rise much higher. Sometimes support or resistance levels are at precisely the same point. Other times they are not so exact but rather are a range of support or resistance.

Keep in mind, these are tendencies, not guarantees. The stock market does what buyers and sellers determine, not necessarily what someone thinks it's supposed to do.

## ONE BECOMES THE OTHER

Resistance becomes support, and support becomes resistance. The two conditions of support and resistance switch roles (Figure 12-1). When resistance is penetrated, resistance becomes support. If the Dow Industrial Average stops a few times at the 10,000 level, then rises to 10,100, the former resistance level becomes support. On the other end, if the market falls through a support area, that area becomes new resistance.

In November 2002 the Dow Industrial Average encountered previously established resistance at 8,996 points. It corrected, dropping until it found support at 7,891 points.

## STOCK PRICES

Stock prices also show areas of support and resistance. In fact, they are a key element in technical analysis and are frequently observed by the fun-

**F I G U R E   12–1**

Dow Industrial Average and Volume, 2002–2004

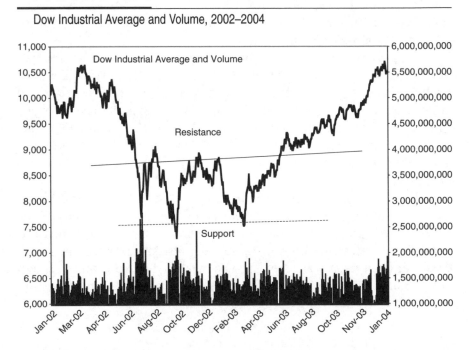

damental analyst. As with indicators, the areas show where buyers or sellers enter the market. In March 2004, Paul Cherney, chief analyst for Standard & Poor's, had this to say about the importance of support in his March 2, 2004 article for *Insight from Standard & Poors*, "Support Levels Are Key":

All the historical studies in the world don't matter if prices do not move in agreement with them. Even though we are in a period of time when recently there has been a history of positive price action, if price is not moving in the same direction as the tendencies quantified in the studies suggest, then the studies do not matter, only prices matter. The support levels mentioned above appear important because neither the Nasdaq nor the S&P 500 was able to establish a higher high, and that means that if there is a close below those support levels, then a series of lower highs and lower lows will have been established, and that is the definition of a downtrend.

## IMPERFECT PREDICTORS

Support and resistance do not really predict or forecast what will happen next. All they do is indicate what happened in the past and could happen again. The anticipation and subsequent actions of buyers and sellers will determine what happens. However, the knowledge of support and resistance can give the investor an indication of what is likely to happen.

### The Example of 3M

Take a look at the price action of 3M (Figure 12-2). Notice how the $60 price level was strong resistance back in 2001 to about April 2002. The price then shifted up a bracket and the resistance that had been so strong became support, to July 2003, where the stock rallied all the way up to $85 a share.

Notice how in July and October 2002 corrections that penetrated the support level tended to fall much further. This is also true of the upside. As resistance is penetrated, a good rally usually ensues.

## THEY ARE IMPORTANT

The understanding of resistance and support, both at the broad market level and the individual stock level, are important to seeing what a price is likely to do. Remember that when a support or resistance level is penetrated, more of the same can be expected, usually (but not always) to the next level of support or resistance.

# FIGURE 12-2

3M Corporation, 2002–2003

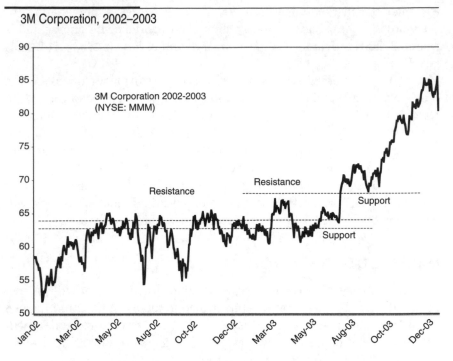

# CHAPTER 13

# There Is a Bear Market Coming

Of course, there is—there is always the specter of a bear market on the economic horizon. It's as true as the fact that some investors believe the Dow Industrial Average will drop below 2,000 again. Many who believe the bear is hiding around the corner don't even have a clear definition of what makes a bear.

## WHAT IS A BEAR MARKET?

Actually, there are several definitions of a bear market.

### A Classic

A bear market is a time when securities prices are steadily declining for a period of weeks, months, and sometimes years.

### Trader Vic's Bear Market

A long-term downtrend (a downtrend lasting months to years) in any market, especially the stock market, characterized by lower intermediate lows (those established in a time frame of weeks to months) interrupted by lower intermediate highs.

### Marty Zweig's Bear

A bear market is a decline of at least 15 percent in each of three important stock averages: the Dow Jones Industrials, the S&P 500 Index, and the … Value Line Index.

### Another Classic

A bear market is a decline in the Dow Industrial Average of 20 percent or more. It can also be a time when the Dow Industrial Average is down (from established highs) for more than two consecutive months.

Keep in mind that newscasters and analysts will talk of "bearish" moves in the stock market. They do not necessarily mean that the stock market has become a bear market. Virtually all corrections or secondary market downtrends are referred to as "bearish."

## WHAT'S THE TREND?

A bear market represents a downturn in the long-term trend. Most of these trends are short-lived. They might last from three to six months. Only a few last more than a year, the most notable being the bear market from October 1929 to July 1932.

One of the problems with the crash of 1929 was the fact that many companies went out of business, either because of the bear market or the economic climate that followed. Most, in 1998, have viewed the economic climate as positive, with this most recent market acceleration. However, there is a problem with the Asian economic crises.

### A Word of Caution

The bear market of 2001 through early 2003 was a well-defined down primary trend. The turn was clear-cut, as was the primary uptrend of 2003 to early 2004 (Figure 13-1). Then things got muddy. A train bombing in Spain and a terrorist threat letter sent the markets into a tailspin that broke down through the uptrend line. Once the primary uptrend line is penetrated, many investors become nervous wondering whether it is just a secondary trend or in fact a real turn in the primary trend.

## THE MARKET DOESN'T USUALLY WAIT

If there is a strong enough belief that a recession is coming, the stock market probably won't wait to send a signal. For that matter, the recession probably won't wait either. Recessions have a tendency to move just ahead of the current economic situation. Although they seem to be always looming in the future, if the right moves are made, the recessions often don't materialize.

## FIGURE 13–1

Dow Industrial Average, March 2001–February 200

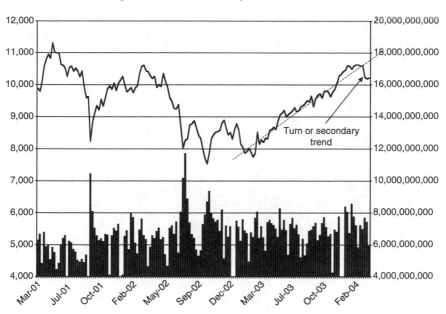

## THE BEAR GROWLS

Comments from an important figure like Federal Reserve Chairman Alan Greenspan can throw the stock market into turmoil. Who benefits from the warnings?

When the Fed acts by raising or lowering interest rates, everyone listens. Actions speak louder than words, and the stock market is most sensitive to changes in interest rates.

## BEAR MARKETS—BUYING OPPORTUNITIES

They certainly have been buying opportunities in the past, with some notable exceptions.

The 1929 bear saw several companies go out of business. The way to avoid such difficulties is to choose stocks carefully and wait for some signs of stability. However, a wait can be difficult because of the speed the market can recover. Waiting too long leads to missed opportunities.

# PART III

# Strategy

The most important part of strategy is setting investment objectives. Each investor should have a well-defined general objective as well as a specific objective for each individual investment. To say, "I want to make a lot of money in the stock market," cannot be considered an objective. It's a dream … a wish without definition. An investment objective must:

- Be specific
- Be reasonable in expectations
- Consider risk
- Have a time frame
- Be measurable

Setting this kind of objective allows the investor to know what is to be achieved, by when, and by how much. The objective can be analyzed periodically to see if achievement is possible. If it is not possible, the investments can be altered to a new objective.

Other fine points of strategy are also examined in this section: selling short, selling short against the box, and deciding which stocks to sell. Diversification as a strategy is also examined. Diversification is limited in what it can do and often doesn't offer as much protection as many people think. The fact is, if the market is in a downtrend, diversification offers little or no protection.

# CHAPTER 14

# Invest According to Objectives

**"I** want to make a lot of money in the stock market, but I don't want to take risks."

Is it a wish or an objective? Since one of the synonyms for the word *objective* is *measurable*, the general statement is assuredly a wish. However, a wish can be redefined as an objective.

## ESTABLISHING A GOOD OBJECTIVE

Often, such things as retirement, children's college education, a house, or a new car are stated as objectives for investing. Even they are quite general, although they're more specific than "a lot of money." What about a set time for achievement? Retirement and children's education have built-in time periods; however, it's a good idea to break these large (10- or 20-year) blocks of time into smaller segments, like one to five years. Having a short time for achievement helps to ensure that the investor evaluates the performance and makes changes along the way.

### Decisions Need to Be Made

In order to meet an investment objective, certain information is essential. What specifically will be done? What performance is reasonable? What kind of stocks will be purchased? How much diversification is necessary to moderate risk? What time frame should be used? How will success be measured? When the answers to these questions are decided, they need to be set down in writing.

An objective should have the following characteristics:

- *Be specific:* What activities will be done to choose investments?
- *Have reasonable expectations:* Base expectations on observable performance.
- *Consider risk:* Select stocks and diversify to a comfort level.
- *Have a time frame:* One year, two years, five years, and so on.
- *Be measurable:* Performance needs to be measured to be evaluated.

## CATEGORIES OF STOCK

When stockbrokers open new accounts, they are required by Rule 144 of the NYSE to know their customer. That means they need to know certain details about the person's investing experience, financial status, and, most important, investment objectives. In order to standardize objectives into mutually understood concepts, they usually list four categories for investment:

- *Income:* Investments that generate income from dividends or interest payments
- *Growth:* Investments that demonstrate price growth—usually newer companies that pay no dividends
- *Total return:* Investments that will see both price growth and income from dividends
- *Speculation:* Investments for short-term trades that result in quick profits (e.g., new companies, companies in rapid growth areas, turnarounds, and other speculative situations)

Income, growth, total return, or speculation—all financial investments fit into these categories.

### Income Stock

Traditionally, income stocks are most often utilities, especially electrical utilities. They are usually conservative investments with steady streams of income, and are typically financially stable. Although there is always risk involved with common stock investing, income stocks should have some of the lowest risk. Sometimes they are colorfully referred to as the "widow and orphan stocks," meaning investments for people who can't afford to lose money.

Obviously, dividends are a priority when an investor's objective is income. Dividend growth and dividend stability are likewise important. Looking at the average annual growth of dividends over at least a five-year period can give the investor some idea of how much growth to expect in the future. In order for a company to pay out dividends, the growth of revenues and income are important.

The primary sources of income can be a concern in some areas. The Detroit area might have trouble if the automotive industry is in a slump. The Silicon Valley area of California might have trouble when the computer industry is slow. The source of income is a part of risk; more specifically, the risk of slower growth.

## Matching the General Objective

With income as a general objective, we will narrow the focus to looking at electric utility companies that have a current yield comparable to five-year U.S. Treasury notes (for example, August 7, 1998, at 5.375 percent). These companies should have somewhat consistent growth in dividend payments, revenues, and earnings.

Once income becomes the objective, select some candidates (five to 10) and choose which you believe to be the best opportunities. We will look at three examples, beginning with Consolidated Edison.

## Consolidated Edison

Consolidated Edison, Inc. (NYSE: ED) owns all of the outstanding common stock of Consolidated Edison Company of New York, Inc. (Con Edison of New York) and Orange and Rockland Utilities, Inc. Con Edison of New York provides electric service in all of New York City (except part of Queens) and most of Westchester County, an approximately 660-square-mile service area with a population of more than 8 million. It also provides gas service in Manhattan, the Bronx, and parts of Queens and Westchester, and steam service in parts of Manhattan. The company's main business segments are the regulated electric, gas, and steam businesses of its utility subsidiaries and the unregulated businesses of its other subsidiaries.

## Dividend Is Important

For an income objective, the most important information here is the current dividend yield of 5 percent. If the shares are purchased at the $44.12

a share, the investor locks in a 5.5 percent yield no matter what happens to the price. That yield will increase as the dividends are increased (usually annually), but that yield can only decrease if the amount of the dividend is lowered.

As the dividend chart in Figure 14-1 illustrates, Con Edison has had a steady and growing dividend for many years. This chart goes all the way back to 1977 and adjusts for two different stock splits, one in 1982 and the other in 1989.

## Peoples Energy

Peoples Energy is a diversified energy company headquartered in Chicago and comprised of five business units: the core business, Gas Distribution; and diversified businesses, Power Generation, Midstream Services, Oil and Gas Production, and Retail Energy Services. The company has serviced gas to residential and business consumers in northeastern Illinois for 150 years.

For the past 10 years Peoples Energy has increased its dividend on a regular basis (Figure 14-2). That is a very positive fact. Good dividend growth and stability are important for income-producing stock. The divi-

## FIGURE   14–1

Dividend Chart for Consolidated Edison

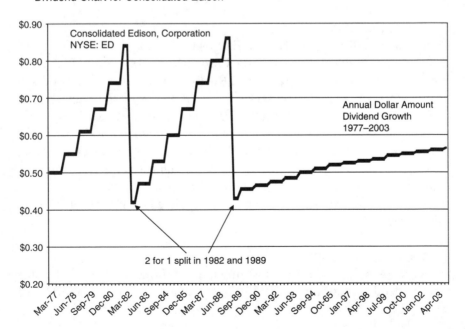

## F I G U R E   14–2

Dividend Chart for Peoples Energy

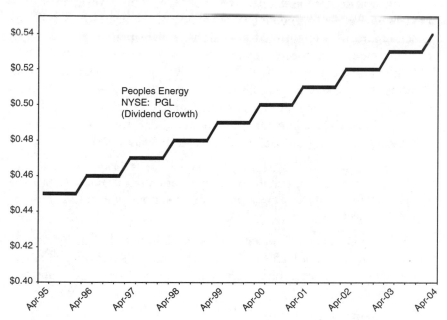

dend at a recent price of $44.63 per share was $2.16, resulting in an annualized yield of 4.81 percent.

## UIL Holdings Corporation

UIL Holdings Corporation is the holding company for the United Illuminating Company (UI) and United Resources, Inc (URI). UI is a New Haven–based regional distribution utility that provides electricity and energy-related services to more than 320,000 customers in municipalities in the Greater New Haven and Greater Bridgeport areas. URI is the umbrella for UIL Holdings' nonutility business units, including American Payment Systems, Inc.; Xcelecom, Inc.; United Capital Investments, Inc.; and United Bridgeport Energy, Inc.[1]

UIL Holdings recently (March 19, 2004) traded at a price of $47.05 per share. At a current annual dividend of $2.88, that's a current yield of 6.11 percent, which beats money markets, CDs, and U.S. Treasuries. It's a yield high enough to worry about. Sure, you want the highest possible

---

[1] UIL Holdings Corporation Web page.

yield with income investing, but you also want that dividend to be secure and not be reduced in the near future.

Notice also that the dividend has not shown any growth since July 1996 (Figure 14-3). This could be a big concern. A quick look at the price chart in Figure 14-4 might shed some light on the situation.

The price chart doesn't really show any unusual problem for UIL Holdings, but the current high yield on the dividend says that investors are unloading the stock or staying away from it at the present time. It bears some additional looking into for possible future problems.

The following comment was made about the company by a Morningstar (Morningstar.com) analyst back in March 2004:

> Over the long haul, this company has posted results that are about average for its industry. Note that the company's net profit margins—another key profitability measure—have been average compared with other companies in its industry.

Stock analysis can be much more thorough than this, depending on how deeply the investor wants to dig into a company's financial situation. Debt, new projects, and future sources of revenue can also be examined.

## FIGURE 14–3

Dividend Chart for UIL Holdings

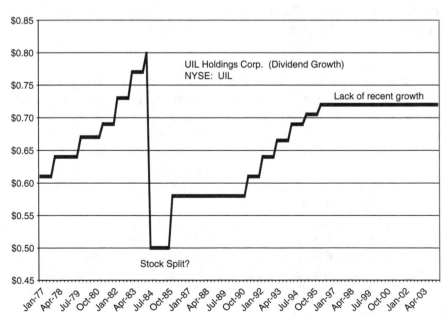

## FIGURE 14–4

Price Chart for UIL Holdings

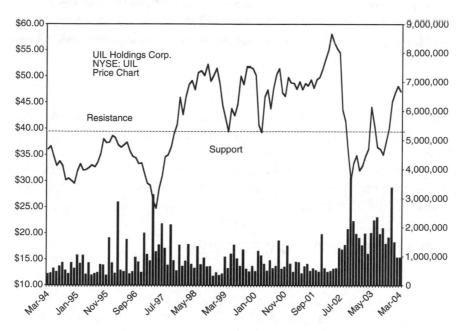

With electric utilities, nuclear and coal issues can be an important area of examination. However, companies that have been consistent in the past will likely continue to be consistent unless an unusual situation arises.

## COMPLETE OBJECTIVE

For purposes of dividend income, we'll say that we've invested $100,000 in the stock of at least three electric utility companies. The expected annual yield will be 4 percent, with at least a 2 percent annual growth rate in the dividend. Risk will be considered by evaluating the consistency of the growth in revenues, earnings, and dividends. Performance will be evaluated at least on an annual basis, with changes made as necessary.

### Evaluation

When an objective is precisely detailed, evaluation is ever so simple. Either the objective is being met or it is not. If not, learn the reason why not, and make a decision to hold your position or sell the stock for a better performing candidate.

Notice that the objective says nothing about price growth. That's because price growth is not a consideration for an income objective. The steady income is important. Any growth in price is just an extra benefit if the investor chooses to sell some or all of the stock. The price growth is often why income investors will choose stock rather than safer U.S. Treasury securities.

### A Short Analysis

The analysis used in this chapter is a brief form of "Fundamental Analysis," examining the revenues, earnings, dividends, and price growth of a company. Even a short analysis tells a lot about a company and its consistent growth. The purpose of this chapter is not to explain analysis, but to illustrate how an analysis can be made based on the information readily available to investors.

## OTHER OBJECTIVE CATEGORIES

### Growth

Investors looking for growth should consider revenue and earnings growth as a higher priority than dividends. Price growth over the past five years essentially replaces dividend growth as a focal point. Growth companies are generally small to midsize, and they are leaders or are becoming leaders in their industry niche. A benchmark for performance can be an index such as the Russell 2,000 Index or the Wilshire 5,000 Index. However, because of the influence of growth stocks on the entire stock market, the investor should also look at the stock's performance within the Dow Industrial Average and the Standard & Poor's 500 Index for growth comparisons.

The price-earnings ratios (P/E ratio equals the price divided by earnings) can be an important part of determining risk in growth stocks, but the ratios should not be examined alone. A current P/E ratio in comparison to a company's five-year average P/E ratio can show whether a stock is currently more or less attractive to buyers. Although it's an oversimplification, a higher than average P/E is considered to indicate more risk, and a lower than average P/E means less risk. It is essential to look at the information behind the P/E ratio and ask why it is high or low. Comparing the P/E ratio to other companies in the same industry can also be helpful in determining risk and market appeal.

For growth stock objectives, look at:

- Price growth
- Revenue growth
- Earnings growth
- Price-earnings ratio (present to five-year average)
- Analyst opinion (Why will the growth continue?)

Growth stock objectives should be evaluated at least annually, but they can also be evaluated quarterly or even monthly. A caution with monthly evaluations: Don't overreact and sell out too soon.

## TOTAL RETURN

Total return stocks are dividend-paying stocks that also have good price growth. The focus is usually on industry leaders, the "stalwarts" that also pay out dividends. These would include the so-called blue-chip stocks like General Electric, 3M, and IBM. They are considered lower-risk stocks because they are well-established companies and because every time a dividend is paid out, the risk is lowered by the amount of each dividend.

Analysis of total return stocks is similar to the analysis for growth stocks, but it will obviously include dividends and dividend growth. The objective statement needs to include both price and dividend growth.

Total return objectives can be evaluated annually, quarterly, or monthly—just be careful with sell decisions. Don't sell out too quickly when the market declines. Often that is the best time to buy more stock.

## SPECULATION

The speculation category covers everything else. It can be the act of investing with "wild abandonment," or it can include some analysis to moderate risk. Although there is a belief among many that higher risk brings higher rewards … this is not usually what happens. Higher risk can also mean greater losses.

Rather than approaching speculative investing with wild abandonment, why not just extend the objective to a higher level. If the Standard & Poor's Index is growing at 10 percent, set the objective at 30 percent, or use a shorter time period for achievement. Use basic fundamental analysis to find companies that either have or are working toward strong revenues and earnings. Technical analysis is also used for short-term speculative investing, but the risk can be moderated by learning some basics about the company.

No matter what type of analysis is used for speculative investing, the greatest difficulty is keeping up with the rapidly changing market. Opportunities appear suddenly and are gone within minutes. The individual investor can have problems trying to keep up with the professionals who watch the market change tick by tick.

Evaluation of speculative trading is often done on trade-by-trade basis.

## WHAT AN OBJECTIVE DOES

Setting a well-defined objective makes investing easier for the investor. Decisions to buy or sell stock are easier because it is only necessary to determine if the stock fits the objective or is achieving the objective. If a stock doesn't fit, don't buy it; if performance is below standard with recovery unlikely, sell.

## REVIEW

An objective should have the following characteristics:

- Specificity
- Reasonable expectations
- A consideration of risk
- A time frame
- Measurability

# CHAPTER 15

# Sell the Losers and
# Let the Winners Run

The title of this chapter is one of the oldest sayings in the stock market. In the late 1800s, Daniel Drew had a slightly different version: "Cut your losses and let your profits run."

The concept is sound; in fact, it is one of the most important understandings an investor can have about the stock market. It is prudent for an investor to sell stocks that are losing money, stocks that could continue to drop in price and value. It makes equally good sense to stay with stocks that show significant gains, as long as they remain fundamentally strong.

But just what is a loser? Is it any price drop from the high? Is a stock a loser only if the investor is actually in a loss position—that is, when the current price is below the original purchase price?

Any price drop is a losing situation. Price drops cost the investor money. They are a loss of profits. In some circumstances the investor should sell, but in other situations the investor should take a closer look before reaching a sell decision.

The determination of whether a stock is still a winner depends on the cause of the price correction. If a price drop occurs because of a weakness in the overall market situation or is the result of a "normal" daily fluctuation of the stock price, the stock can still be a winner.

If, however, the cause of the drop has long-term implications, it could be time to take the loss and move on to another stock. Long-term implications could be any of the following:

- Declining sales
- Tax difficulties
- Legal problems
- An emerging bear market
- Higher interest rates
- Negative impacts on future earnings

Any event that has a negative impact on the long-term picture of earnings or earnings growth can quickly turn a stock into a loser. Many long- and short-term investors will sell out their positions and move on to a potential winner.

### AT&T Became a Loser

Hard to believe that one of the most popular stocks in the United States could fall out of favor and become a loser. But that's exactly what happened in the fall of 2001, when its price trend began to pull away from the winning stocks. The divergence continued through 2002, and even into 2003. See Figure 15-1. Finally, in March 2003 it started to look like a good stock again.

## VALUE IN EARNINGS GROWTH

Value, in terms of growth potential, is based on earnings and earnings growth. Analysis of earnings and news about a company can give some insight into the quality of earnings. If management has increased earnings by firing half the company's personnel, or the increase is derived from closing several facilities, the quality of the increase is not as valuable as it would be if it reflected improved sales and other revenues. Slash-and-burn strategies can lead to a further decline in productivity, resulting in additional weakness in earnings and eventually lower prices for the stock. On the positive side, drastic cuts can force companies to become more efficient, thereby increasing the quality of earnings, which may lead to higher stock prices.

The investor must analyze the company's growth and observe the stock price in action. From the analysis, the investor can determine whether the value of a stock is more likely to increase, remain flat, or begin to decline. The analysis can be difficult at times because a winner can temporarily take on the appearance of a loser.

Three situations—daily price fluctuations, market declines, and price advances followed by weaknesses—can make a winner appear to

**F I G U R E  15–1**

AT&T and Dow Industrial Average, April 2001–February 2004

look weak, but they are not necessarily a signal to begin selling. These are usually temporary situations and are therefore exceptions to the sell-the-losers rule.

## Exception 1: Daily Price Fluctuations

Stock prices fluctuate up or down in day-to-day trading. A glance at any daily price chart will show what may be considered normal daily fluctuations for any individual stock (see Figure 15-2). Stock prices also move from one trading range to another. For example, a stock price could have a daily fluctuation of $30 to $35 but could occasionally move to $40 and then drop back to the $30 to $35 range. The trading range would be considered $30 to $40. When the stock moves up and begins fluctuating between $40 and $55, it is trading in a new, higher range.

The stock of NCR Corp. followed the Dow Industrial Average rather nicely from 2001 through early 2004. Small areas of divergence appear,

**F I G U R E   15–2**

Trading Comparison, NCR Corp. and the Dow Industrials, April 2001–January 2004

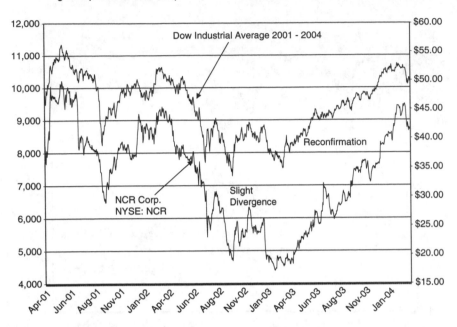

but are minor. Clearly, the weaknesses of NCR are related to the entire stock market.

The trading ranges and daily fluctuations can be readily observed on a price pattern chart. The investor should take the time to become familiar with these trading ranges and fluctuations from the preceding few months. Many Internet sources provide daily price charts at no charge. They can be saved on a computer or printed (where allowed). Familiarity with price movements will help the investor differentiate between a normal fluctuation and a breakout to a new trading range. If a lower stock price is within the normal range, it may still be a winner, even if the investor is experiencing a small loss—assuming that the initial analysis showed the stock to be a winner in earnings and growth. Therefore, the kind of weakness seen in a normal fluctuation does not indicate that the time to sell out and take a loss has arrived.

### Exception 2: Market Decline

On October 19, 1987, more than 604 million shares were traded on the New York Stock Exchange and 239 million on the American and Nasdaq (over-the-counter) markets, shattering previous records. Investors lost more than $500 billion in stock market value, according to Wilshire Associates of Los Angeles, which publishes an index of some 6,000 publicly traded stocks.

A significant drop in the overall stock market can force the price of a winner to lower levels. All stocks can eventually look like losers, and some will become losers. Most often these severe market corrections are a time for concern, but not panic. As we have seen in recent years, the stock market can drop 100, 200, or more than 500 points and recover quickly. Stocks that were winners before the correction will likely be winners again when the market recovers.

In October 1987 the Dow Industrials dropped more than 508 points (22.6 percent). Looking back in 2004, that is still the largest percentage drop in one day. Figure 15-3 illustrates what happened to Merck & Company on October 19, which at the time was the biggest one-day drop in history. Merck had already been showing some weakness, but on the sharp correction, it dropped a significant $1.50. This correction was an overall market reaction. For Merck, the weakness of the market in late

## FIGURE 15–3

Market Correction, Merck & Company, January–November 1987

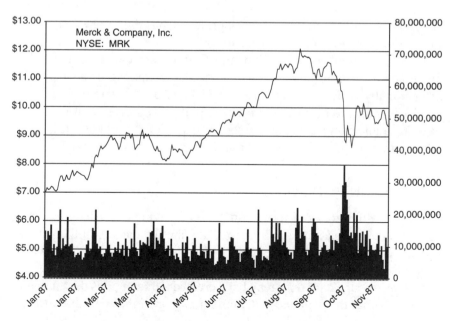

1987 was an excellent buying opportunity. It began a quick recovery, and by April 1988, after prices were adjusted for a stock split, Merck was trading above $9.00 a share.

## In a Continuing Decline

If the market correction is sudden and appears to stabilize in just a few days, it may be best to hold a position and even consider buying more shares of the same stock. Many investors recognized the severe correction in 1987, for example, as a buying opportunity. Although the Dow remained volatile, it reached new highs in early 1989.

Unless they are severe and extend over a few weeks and months, market corrections do not necessarily turn winners into losers. If a market decline continues, however, the investor should consider selling and moving the funds to the sideline. Extended market corrections are bear markets where stock prices decline and interest rates rise.

### Exception 3: Price Advance Followed by a Weakness

A significant upward move to a new trading range, followed by some price weakness, is a fairly normal occurrence. As a stock price makes a major upward movement, many investors will begin to take profits. Although there is nothing wrong with taking profits, the upward price movement might have only just started. Even so, it is inevitable that some profit taking will occur, and the stock price that has risen to new highs will show some downward price correction

A signal is given if a stock begins to fall lower than its daily trading range and the overall market is unchanged or advancing. If a stock price that normally trades between $45 and $50 a share drops to $43 and then to $40, it is time to be concerned. The signal is even stronger if the stocks of comparable companies are not showing a similar weakness. It is a signal to either sell the stock or find out the reason for the price decline.

## CONSISTENT GROWTH

Winners are the stocks of those companies showing consistent growth in revenues (sales), earnings, and price. They are the leaders in their industry and have continual new product developments for new or existing markets. Their products are not passing fads.

Even though a product may have created a tremendous demand, how likely is it that this demand will remain strong in the next three to five

## FIGURE 15–4

Dow Industrial Average, January 2003–February 2004

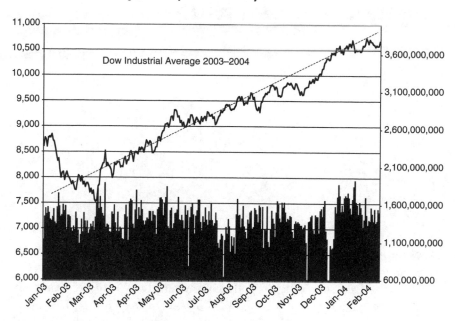

years? Pet Rocks, wall walkers, and Cabbage Patch dolls can have strong sales for a year or two, but seldom can this type of product build enduring demand. Although faddish products can be earnings boosters for well-established companies, they are usually not a firm enough foundation on which to build an entire company.

## FUNDAMENTALS

Winners should be held until the fundamentals that make them winners begin to weaken or until the price runs too far ahead of the earnings, causing a decline in value. Stocks trade on the anticipation of future growth. At times the anticipation vastly outpaces the growth and even the growth potential. Add the news of weaker earnings to that anticipation and the stock price gets hammered down hard. The winner stock becomes a loser.

Losers are taking money from the investor and should be sold and forgotten until they stabilize and rebuild the fundamental strength necessary to be winners..

# CHAPTER 16

# Buy Low, Sell High

**B**ack in the early days of Wall Street, it was stated, "Buy that which is cheap and sell that which is dear."

Charles Dow, one of the founding fathers of Dow Jones & Company and the first managing editor of the *Wall Street Journal*, might have put it this way: "Buy a stock that has value in earnings and value in the dividend paid out. As this stock rises in price and the value of earnings and dividends declines, sell the stock."

Although the methods of evaluating stocks "of value" may have changed, the basic idea is still sound. The anticipation of value and value growth are what make a stock price rise. The value is not the price alone. However, it is one of the factors in determining value. Another important factor of value is earnings past and earnings forecast. Stock prices move in anticipation of future earnings growth.

## AN OLD IDEA

The idea of "buy low, sell high" is as old as trading ownership of properties. It is the basis of all business. Buy a property at one price and sell it at a higher price. The difference between the buy and sell transactions is *profit*. To make a profit is the reason to buy and sell stock.

It is the one axiom almost everyone understands but many have trouble doing. An investor hears that Company ABC is buying out XYC Company. The stock had been trading at $24.50 a share, but the buyout is expected to be at $28.00. The investor knows there is some risk involved and so decides to think about buying 100 shares. The following afternoon the investor calls the broker and learns that XYZ Company is now trading at $30.00. A feeling of panic overcomes the investor because the price is above the buyout price already. Better place that buy order. An order to buy 100 shares of XYZ Company is placed and filled at $27.50 a share.

The following week the investor calls the broker to check on XYZ Company and learns that it is now trading at $25.50. That's a $2 loss per share. Even more frightening, it's a 10 percent loss. Trying to restrain the feeling of panic, the investor gives instructions to sell the 100 shares of XYZ Company at the market. The order is entered and executed at $25.25.

A few weeks later the investor decides to look at the price quote in the newspaper and is shocked to find the stock closed yesterday at $26.50 a share. The investor feels disappointed and exasperated about investing.

Sound Exaggerated?

It isn't, really.

In fact, this scenario could have occurred with Disney in early 2004, when Comcast was trying to buy them out (see Figure 16-1).

## What Went Wrong?

Several things.

When the investor first heard about the takeover, it was already late in the game to make a play. Thinking for a day or two about buying or selling can sometimes be disastrous. The investor sold out the position without learning the details.

Once a strategy is put in play, an investor should not be so quick to change. The investor should have checked the background on the two companies. The 10 percent loss strategy is just that, a 10 percent loss. It has nothing to do with how a price will perform in the next few days. Some professional investors look for stocks that are down 10 to 15 percent and consider them buying opportunities. They know the 10 percenters (with weak hands) will be bailing out and the stock prices can become even better bargains. These investors will allow a 10, 15, or even 20 percent drop (and sometimes more) because the majority of buyers did not buy at the top.

- If an investor is going to speculate on takeovers, it is important that he or she realize that the prices will tend to be volatile until the actual takeover occurs.

## FIGURE 16–1

Walt Disney Company, December 2003–March 2004

- The axiom "buy low, sell high" should not be followed in reverse by the investor.

## WHY NOT THE CYCLICALS?

If an investor wants to buy low and sell high on the same stock, why not go to the cyclicals, such as automobile stocks? When they cycle down, buy. When they cycle up, sell. The only trick is to understand when the change is coming. Take a look at General Motors in Figure 16-2.

It looks like a no brainer. Buy in the trough below $45.00 and sell on the peak above $55.00. What could be easier?

Car companies are simple. You build a car, you sell a car. Build too many and there are problems. Don't sell enough and there are problems. But the basic business is not complicated; it's a simple commodity. As a manufacturer, you have only two concerns: the competition and the old "beater" the consumer is now driving. Sales bounce back and forth depending on who has the greatest bells and whistles or occasionally who has the best knock-your-socks-off warranty, which the manufacturer will regret.

In the 1990s car manufacturers did an excellent job of attracting customers with stock features: the safety items, air bags, and antilock brakes.

## FIGURE  16–2

General Motors, April 2001–January2004

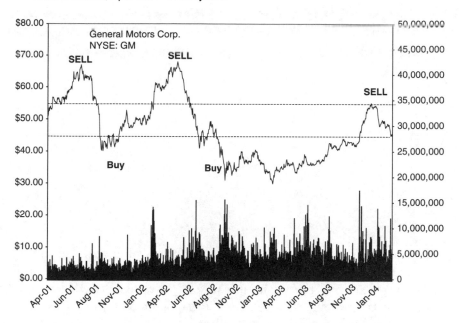

They also invested in appearance items such as cool colors, mag wheels, and wide tires (remember white walls?). They have made available all sizes of pickups and sports utility vehicles (probably the most effective marketing).

Megadollars have been spent to encourage the consumer to buy the latest and best vehicle from Ford, General Motors, and Chrysler. These companies have all consistently done well at bringing in the dollars. The public has benefited by having better cars. The companies have benefited by having greater profits. The stock buyer has benefited by owning a winning stock. So, who lost? Well, there were a few thousand workers put out of work by consolidation and automation. In some cases this was catastrophic, but in most it was recoverable. Change is inevitable, and our society is gradually waking up to the knowledge that it can be a good thing.

In using the simple buy low, sell high trading strategy, if fundamentally good companies are carefully selected, the rewards from stock ownership can be good and sometimes great. It may take some time and patience for the stock to perform well, but it is often worth the wait. Some companies have income and earnings growing with or ahead of the price. In these situations the axiom of buy low, sell high might be changed to "buy low, buy high, and don't sell."

# CHAPTER 17

# Buy High, Sell Higher

Many individuals are attempting to "buy high and sell higher" when they buy a stock that is on the move. In fact, professional traders frequently use the strategy. Soaring prices are attractive to investors, who believe the prices will keep moving. As long as the momentum of the price swing attracts new buyers, the soaring stock price will continue to climb. It might run up for a couple of days, weeks, or even months. Eventually, however, there is a hesitation, followed by a turn as the profit taking begins. The last buyers not only have the smallest gains from the run up, they will obviously also have the biggest losses. It's somewhat like a pyramid scheme where the losers are the last to join.

A severe market decline creates lower prices and large cash positions even though the earnings of stocks can remain unchanged (meaning that their value is increasing as prices decline). The bargains can be resisted for only a limited time. In a severe market decline, the climb back to former levels could take a few months or longer, but the recovery will come in time.

## WHERE ARE THE PLAYS?

Individual investors can seek out stocks that are either in play by the institutions or are likely to come into play. Often they are stocks with strong fundamentals in earnings and revenues, found in industries with good growth potential. In the late 1990s computer software companies with products related to the Internet showed great potential. Medical products and devices can be exciting fast-growth companies. Sometimes older products companies with strong growth records do well.

## Gannett Company, Inc.

Take a look at the price movement of Gannett stock in Figure 17-1. A glance at the price chart shows strong price growth, in line with the stock market. Growth was especially strong in the 2001 and late 2003. The price went from the low 50s to more than $80 a share. Volume increased also just more buyers than sellers.

On the way up there were several areas of weakness, dips in price that turned out to be excellent buying opportunities. In 2002 there was an opportunity at about the $70 level. And along the way there were several $8 or $9 dips that provided some excellent buying opportunities.

## F I G U R E   17–1

Gannett Company, January 1999–April 2004

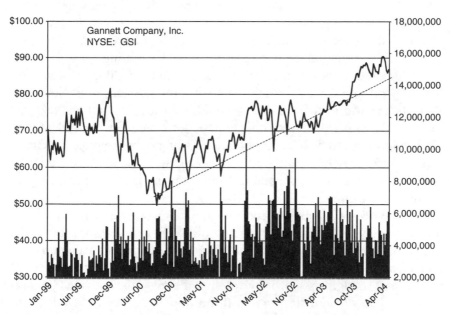

## ENHANCEMENTS

The strategy of buy high, sell higher can be enhanced by anticipated increases in earnings or by corporate takeover situations. Although anticipation of higher earnings creates unusually high P/E ratios, when the earnings do increase, the ratios return to normal levels. If the earnings do not cause a return to normal levels, sellers will eventually force the return. As the price drops, so will the P/E ratio.

## TAKEOVERS

Corporate takeovers create a different situation. Professional arbitrageurs go on search missions in which they look specifically for companies likely to be bought out by some other company. In the late 1980s there were several large leveraged buyout (LBO) situations. The LBO takeover can become a classic buy high, sell higher situation. For those companies who could arrange the deals, there was less risk with greater profits.

## LONG-TERM INTENTION

Buying high and selling higher can be a viable way to make money in the stock market, but it is not without risk. The strategy usually calls for the intention of a longer-term hold—for example, when the earnings cannot catch up with the price, or, in a takeover, when the deal is finalized. Although it is possible to trade in and out during volatile times, the whipsaw effects of being on the wrong side can be devastating.

Corporate takeovers that fail to materialize are a different story. If a buyout does not occur, the stock price will probably fall to previous levels or below. Most often, investors would be prudent to sell and take the loss quickly, rather than hang on and hope for a recovery. A prudent play after selling out can be to attempt bottom fishing once the price gets hammered. Such activity should be based on the individual's belief that the stock can weather the storm and that the company is still capable of generating good earnings.

It would not be unusual for institutional or other experienced stock traders to play these stocks for small profits. They might sell short at the peaks and attempt to buy long at the lows. Such actions often end up to be momentum oriented. They watch the trades minute by minute to see if there is any strength as shown by volume. If strength is indicated by larger volume, they hold their position. If the volume declines, they close out their positions and plan their next strategy. Obviously, timing is everything in these speculative strategies.

## LONG OR SHORT TERM

Buy high, sell higher can work for either the conservative long-term or speculative short-term strategy. But what either strategy needs is a stock that has a solid reason to go higher in price. Two of the main reasons for a stock price to go higher are anticipated higher earnings or a takeover plan.

# CHAPTER 18

# Sell High, Buy Low

Sell short at a high price and buy back at a lower price. Wonderful, an investor can make money in a falling market. If XYZ Corporation has trouble breaking through price resistance at $50 a share, chances are that many speculators are going to be selling short between $45 and $49, higher if possible. If the price of XYZ falls back to $36 and the investor who sold short at $46 buys it back, that's a profit of $10 a share when the short is closed. The strategy can be profitable in the right situation; however, there are considerations to be aware of to protect a short position.

## LIMITED GAIN

A short position can profit only to the amount that a price drops (obviously, a stock price cannot drop below zero dollars). But in a short position, there is virtually unlimited risk because there is no limit to how high a stock price can go. Eventually, the shares must be bought back, or, if the investor currently owns the shares, delivered to cover the short position. The potential problem is that if the price doesn't fall, it might rise higher than the investor can afford to pay. Perhaps a verse attributed to Daniel Drew, in the late 1800s, which we quoted in the Preface, expresses the risk more clearly: "He who sells what isn't his'n, buys it back or goes to prison."

## MARGIN CALL

There exist some controls over short selling because a *margin call* can be issued when the price rises to a certain level. A margin call is a brokerage firm's request for money or other marginable securities to be deposited immediately. The call helps to control the risk of the investor and the brokerage firm. Risk can be seriously escalated if a takeover announcement appears relating to the company in which an investor has a short position.

Since a short seller of stock has an obligation to buy back the stock at some point, the broker does not normally permit the short seller to withdraw proceeds. In fact, the firm could require the short seller to deposit a further sum of money or marginable securities in case the stock price rises and additional funds are needed to buy back the stock. All of this is determined by the situation existing in the investor's margin account.

## BORROWED STOCK

This can create situations that are quite annoying when they suddenly appear as problems. In order to prevent a situation in which more shares are sold short than exist, shares must be "borrowed" by the brokerage firm to cover a short sale. If the shares can't be borrowed from within the firm, an attempt is made to borrow the stock from another firm. Sometimes there is a shortage of stock to borrow and the investor is unable to sell short.

Lenders of stock for short positions can call back the stock at any time. If stock cannot be borrowed elsewhere, the position can be closed out by the brokerage firm, no matter what the current profit or loss situation looks like. The short seller is notified, though not necessarily before the stock is repurchased. The borrowing situation means that it is good to select a candidate with a fairly large number of outstanding shares.

Although shares for borrowing can become scarce with any company, the more shares that are outstanding, the more shares there are available for borrowing.

## PRICE IMPLICATIONS

All short selling—except "short against the box," where the investor owns the same stock being sold short—is considered risky speculation. There are usually more forces at work trying to push the price higher than lower. It becomes very high speculation with low-priced stock. Although the lower prices attract many investors, the risk is often much higher than the potential reward. A stock price can drop only to zero, so a $5 or even $10 price doesn't have much further to go. Even though the volatility is often higher in the low-priced stocks, the return potential is quite limited.

It makes sense, especially for someone new to selling short, to start with stock that has a price with some room to fall, although the price will depend partly on the investor's funds available to meet the margin account requirements.

### AT&T Short Selection

The five-year chart of AT&T in Figure 18-1 shows one of the situations many investors would look for as a short sell. After a rather dramatic rise in 1998, the price of AT&T stock seemed to run into a brick wall in the mid-$300 area. It had trouble rising higher in January 1999 through 2000. It was a correction waiting to happen. Finally, in April 2000, the price moved down and crossed the trend line. Then the bottom fell out.

## STRONG MARKET, SLOWER ECONOMY

Selling short tends to increase when the markets are rising rapidly but the national economy isn't growing in a similar manner. Under such conditions, sooner or later there will be a correction in the market, a sudden drop. One can find the volume of short selling in most financial periodicals (especially the *Wall Street Journal*) under "Short Interest Highlights." *Short interest*

### FIGURE 18-1

AT&T, January 1998–March 2004

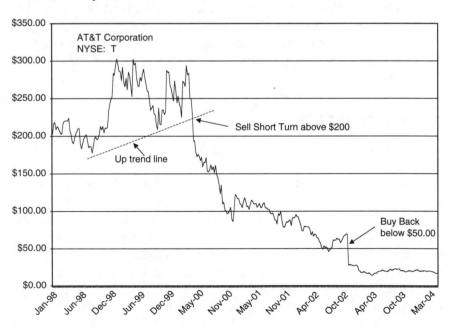

refers to shares that have been sold short. Many investors use the information as a sentiment indicator of strength or weakness in the stock prices.

## SHORT INTEREST ON THE INTERNET

Information on short interest can be obtained from various sources on the Internet. Using a search engine, just typing in the words "short interest" will bring up several pages. The following is an example of a short interest report from the New York Stock Exchange. Over-the-counter short interest can also be obtained on the Internet at nasd.com, which makes the data available on a monthly basis.

### Short Interest Information

Table 18-1 gives a brief sample of some of the data released monthly by the New York Stock Exchange. Data are normally released four to five days after midmonth.

Selling short between $200 and $290 a share would have done well as a strategy if the investor had been able to buy back below $50. A profit of $240 or $150 a share is attractive to the speculator, but problems can arise with selecting a stock based on high levels of short interest.

Should heavy short interest be avoided?

Knowing how short a stock has been sold can be a factor in deciding on a strategy to implement. If too many people short a stock and all attempt to cover their position at the same time, the flurry of buying activity will drive the price up—making it difficult for the individual investor to cover the short position

## SQUEEZE

Sometimes too much short activity can attract large buyers. Buyers know that the short positions will be covered if the stock price rises enough, and that the covering will push the price even higher. Such actions are commonly referred to as a *short squeeze*. If they happen, it's more often by accident than intent. Intentional short squeezes are considered a form of price manipulation and are technically illegal, but it is difficult to prove such intent in a bull market.

## THE UPTICK RULE

An additional word of caution to the short seller: Short sells on a stock exchange can be executed only on an "uptick"(price higher than the previous trade) or "zero-plus tick" (price the same as the last trade, if the last trade was an uptick). The purpose of this rule is to make short selling difficult when a stock price or the market is falling. At the present time, over-the-counter (Nasdaq) stocks are not bound by this uptick rule.

### T A B L E   18-1

September 2004, Top 10 Positions Short Interest Table*

| Symbol | Description | Current Short Pos. | Previous. Short Pos. | Ave. Daily Volume |
|--------|-------------|--------------------|----------------------|-------------------|
| LU  | Lucent Technologies | 268,637,640 | 271,297,910 | 31,570,850 |
| CPN | Calpine Corporation | 118,749,142 | 123,502,212 | 5,331,100 |
| F   | Ford Motor Company  | 94,850,157  | 100,117,800 | 7,167,927 |
| TWX | Time Warner Inc.    | 70,096,162  | 70,750,501  | 9,375,205 |
| DAL | Delta Air Lines, Inc. | 65,142,009 | 61,605,851 | 4,929,941 |
| TYC | Tyco Intl. Ltd.     | 59,524,645  | 59,704,959  | 8,365,759 |
| AMD | Advanced Micro Dev. | 58,638,626  | 58,736,806  | 7,565,723 |
| FON | Sprint Corp.        | 56,484,200  | 59,858,427  | 3,976,100 |
| AMR | AMR Corp.           | 54,072,816  | 50,261,243  | 4,234,923 |
| MU  | Micron Technology   | 51,916,603  | 52,477,436  | 8,362,832 |

*Source: NYSE, Market Information, Data Library, October 11, 2004.

# CHAPTER 19

# Never Short the Trend

*S*horting the trend refers to selling short when a new high is reached in the stock market or by an individual stock price when the trend has been definitely upward. The investor is making a large gamble that the market will turn and decline.

## LOOK FOR THE TURN

Stock prices tend to move as a group, and trends continue until they violate the trend and turn. Shorting a stock at the "top" is generally an exercise in futility and can become costly if an uptrend continues. For individual stocks, a top might be the beginning of a takeover that will push the price even higher. Although it is not a good idea to short the trend, shorting the turn can be profitable.

### Kohl's Incorporated

Kohl's Incorporated (Figure 19-1) had a strong uptrend going from April 1999 until June 2001. Then a strong violation of the trend occurred; even the trend violation could have been a short sell scenario. But the best short finally came in May 2002, where the trend turned from a strong uptrend to a definite downtrend. A short sale at $70.00 a share was not unreasonable. Closing the short out at $50.00 or less would not have been difficult.

## FIGURE 19–1

Kohl's Incorporated, April 1999–April 2004

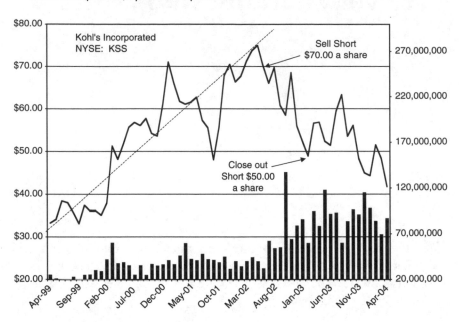

## WEEKLY CHART

Look at the weekly chart of Freeport-McMoran Copper & Gold (FCX) in Figure 19-2. In weekly charts a lot of important detail can be lost, but if they are compared to daily charts, they can also give a better idea of the strength and duration of a trend. On the weekly chart we see a long-term uptrend for FCX. Although there was some volatility, the turn didn't appear until the end of April 2003. The trend violation in August was minor.

As can be seen, FCX had a well-defined turn in the trend in April through December 2003. When the turn came in December, it was well-defined. It's a fairly safe bet that considerable short selling occurred in December 2003 and January 2004. There were actually two short sell opportunities. The first turn could have shorted between $45 and $40 and closed out about $36. The second turn could have shorted between $42 and $40 and closed out somewhere around $30 a share.

In most cases not much is lost by using weekly chart data as opposed to daily data. Obviously, if a major event occurs on a day not included in

## FIGURE 19–2

Trend, Freeport-McMoran Copper & Gold, April 2003–April 2004

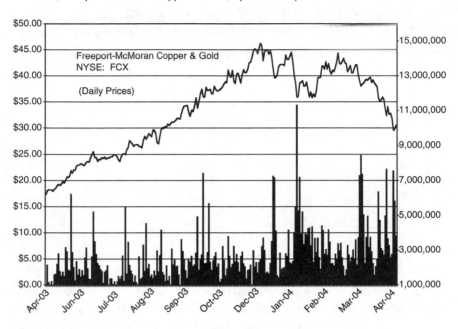

the weekly it will be missed. But weekly data can be used for most trend line establishments and turning point areas.

## NEVER SHORT THE TREND—SHORT THE TURN

Selling short is a risky way of investing. It should be approached with caution, and with knowledge of the company and its price trend. Buy stop orders can be used for upside protection, but they cannot substitute for vigilance in study and observation. Short selling is most often pursued on a short-term basis, before the stock drops low enough to become attractive to buyers or another company with takeover plans.

# CHAPTER 20

# Make Winners Win Big

It was Jessie Livermore, known for his aggressive investing at the turn of the century, who indicated the importance of winning big. When the investor's conclusions, based on analysis, are correct, it's time to win big. Livermore did this when he sold short shares of Union Pacific Railroad just before the 1906 San Francisco earthquake. At first the price did not drop. The company was strong and the price held. After all, it was one of the best companies on Wall Street. Livermore believed it would take a few weeks for the news to spread and the implications of the news to be realized, and he put his fortune on the line, expecting as much. Eventually, he was proven right and his fortune multiplied significantly. He believed in winning big when he knew he was right.

## VALUE

Winning stocks are a special situation. Although it is prudent to establish a price objective for a winning stock, value also needs to be considered before selling. *Value* is the price appreciation in relation to the fundamental growth of the company (e.g., earnings and revenues). The momentum of anticipation can cause a company's stock price to run ahead of earnings potential. Sometimes the earnings potential backfills the price growth, and sometimes it doesn't.

More than one investment adviser is guilty of saying, "When you make 100 percent or 200 percent on a stock, sell and take the profit. Leave something for the next investor." Livermore didn't believe in such a strategy, most institutional investors surely do not follow that practice, and it's a cinch that Warren Buffett doesn't sell because of the amount of profit in a stock. So why should anyone else sell, just when the action gets interesting?

## PROFITS LEFT ON THE TABLE

Any sustained bull market will give examples of stock that should not have been sold even though the price may have doubled, tripled, or even quadrupled. Significant profits are frequently "left on the table" as a misguided investor sells to take profits too soon.

Say for example you got real lucky and bought Ball Corporation (Figure 20-1), the packaging company, at $15 a share back in October 2000. Please note that the price was not actually that low. The $15 also includes a two for one forward split in February 2002 (S). But effectively you paid the $15 per share price tag. You bought a thousand shares and put out $15,000 plus some commission.

### FIGURE 20-1

Ball Corporation, April 1999–March 2004

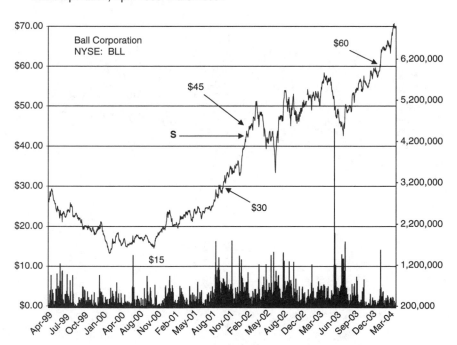

You could have sold the stock in October 2001 and made a 100 percent gain on your investment. Later, you could have sold in March 2002 and made 200 percent on you original investment. Or you could have sold in January 2004 and made 400 percent on your original investment. Knowing all that, would you still want to sell when you doubled your money? I don't think so. So forget the nonsense about selling and taking profits when it's not necessary.

Only two things can make it necessary:

1. You need the money for something else.
2. You believe that the growth potential of the stock has changed.

When you get a stock that is winning, let it win as big as it can. Avoid chopping the legs out from under it by selling too soon to take profits. It's the losers you want to sell, not the winners. If you're in business, you don't fire your best employees; and if you're an investor, don't sell your best stocks.

# CHAPTER 21

# Buy on the Rumor, Sell on the News

**A**n old saying that usually accompanies the buy high, sell higher strategy is to "buy on the rumor, sell on the news." This can be an effective strategy in many ways, but the investor must be aware of the circumstances. For instance, the rumor might have been fabricated with the intent of pushing the stock price up.

Financial consultants, advisers, or stockbrokers tend to discourage those who would buy any stock based on rumor. False rumors frequently appear regarding corporate takeover situations. The share prices advance, but then suddenly retreat to former levels. In most situations it is best to leave the rumor alone. In fact, buying "on the news" can be appealing at times. Perhaps a better refinement would be: Do not wait for the buyout to occur.

## THINGS CHANGE

Although back in the 1980s the tire company Firestone had a takeover offer at $40, which was sweetened to $70 by a new suitor, such increases are rare and have not occurred in more recent years. Northwest Airlines had a takeover offer increased by a new suitor. Back then, selling on the news was selling too soon. Now, it might make more sense. For example, take Disney.

According to Figure 21-1, an investor might have bought Disney at $23 or $24 a share and sold on the news at $28, making a $4 or $5 per share gain in a couple of days. However, notice that there is not much time to make these decisions. The price quickly runs up and immediately starts to decay. Obviously, "sell on the news" means right away.

## TARGET PRICE

When takeover details are announced, the market price of the target company will usually rise to, or close to, the new market value, the value of the acquisition. Many investors sell their holdings at this point instead of waiting for the actual takeover. Although they might not receive the full acquisition value, their assets aren't tied up while waiting for the deal to be completed. Also, they don't lose out if the acquisition fails to materialize.

## SPECULATIVE STRATEGY

Buying on rumor and selling on or after news is high speculation. Things change, and takeovers can fail to occur. Rumors reach the news media

## FIGURE 21–1

Walt Disney Company, December 2003–May 2004

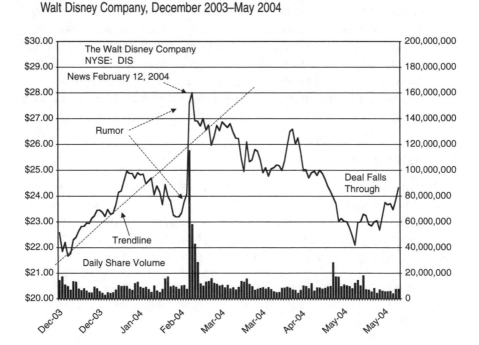

after the action has started. Often, this is too late for the individual investor. Many sophisticated investors avoid rumor investing because of the uncertainty. It is more prudent to look for companies that might become attractive takeover candidates and have other desirable traits. Then, if these companies are not taken over, the investor still has a quality stock at a good price.

# CHAPTER 22

# Buy the Stock That Splits

"This stock split two for one at $40 a share and ran up to $40 again, all within six months. It's just incredible how fast this company is growing. The stock is now at $42 a share, and there's talk of another two-for-one split. It's been great to have more stocks like this one."

This is obviously the sound of a happy investor. *Stock splits* are looked upon as being good news because the price will often continue to increase, given time. However, even though many stock splits are positive, sadly, that is not always the case. Many times the price will soar for the split, only to fall back to previous price levels, adjusted to the split.

## MECHANICS OF A SPLIT

Stock dividends and splits have basically three occurrences: announcement date, record date, and payment date. To qualify for the split, the investor must be the owner on the record date (similar to the ex-date for dividends). Therefore, the stock must be purchased at the appropriate time before the record date to qualify.

### Announcement Date

This can be considered the most important date because it tends to have the greatest positive impact on a stock's price. Even companies that do not react well to a split tend to move initially higher on the announcement.

Rumors of a split sometimes leak out ahead of the announcement date, which also tends to push the price higher.

Stock split and stock dividend announcements are given to the media (including the Internet) on the announcement date. The company provides all the important details of the split and often a brief history of the company's previous stock splits, which it sends out in the form of a press release. The company considers a forward stock split a positive event and wants to get as much free media publicity as possible.

### 3M's Positive Split Story

The 3M Corporation announced a two-for-one forward split on August 11, 2003. The effective price per share at that time was $70.95. By December 22, 2003, another $15 was added to that price. On 100 shares, that's $1,500; and on 1,000 shares, it's obviously $15,000, not a bad gain for four months. Was it the split alone? No, since the Dow was up 188 points, which didn't hurt. But the Dow's increase was not responsible for the entire 3M gain.

## PRICE WEAKNESS

It is not unusual to see some price weakness either after a split announcement or shortly after a payment date. Any number of things can cause a price to drop. For example, speculators could be exiting and taking profits, especially if the price has been flat for a time. Some investors might fear that the price action is over and expect a drop, and they would rather sell too soon than too late. Obviously, others see this price weakness as a buying opportunity, and they are the investors who drive the price upward.

## THEY DON'T ALWAYS GO UP

### Kronos and ADC Telecommunications

Kronos Incorporated stock split three for two in October 2003, and the stock didn't do much of anything. The price rose from $37.00 to nearly $41.00 a share, then dropped like a rock, closing out March 2003 at $32.50. A short chance to make $3 or $4 a share and then go to a losing situation, the Nasdaq index didn't appear to offer any assistance to the price in this specific situation (Figure 22-1).

# FIGURE 22–1

Kronos Incorporated, January 1999–April 2004

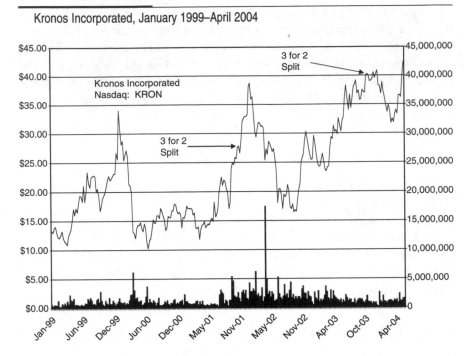

Back in 2000, ADC Telecommunications had two splits, one in February and another in October. The price surged to an effective $45 a share. That was a possible $5 per share gain on the second split, and a whopping $24 per share gain on the first split, way back in February of that year. But there was a problem. After the second split, the stock went into a steep dive that took it below $3 a share. It still lingered there in 2004.

It's usually not the split that gets a company into trouble. More likely it's the reason for the split. If the company is trying to use the split to be positive in the face of forthcoming negative information, the positive spin doesn't hold up for long. Investors, whether professional or nonprofessional, will come to realize the truth of the situation and react accordingly—by selling the stock.

## WHY COMPANIES HAVE STOCK SPLITS

Ordinarily, the reason a company decides to split its stock is to make it more attractive for investors to purchase. The logic is that more people will buy the stock at $30 rather than $60. Obviously, as more people buy the stock at the lower price, the stock will rise in price. The split makes the stock more affordable to individual investors.

Whereas a $120 price might be too high for many, a $60 or even $30 price will get them to buy the stock. However, there is no assurance that stock will continue to rise in price after the split. Often, a stock price declines in price after a split, which can be true particularly if a stock splits more than once in a year.

Another reason for a company to have a stock split is to make more shares available, thereby broadening its stockholder base. The stock becomes somewhat more marketable and liquid. Somehow, positive publicity also fits into the stock split scenario. A company might use a stock split announcement to soften the blow of some negative news. On the other side of that coin, a company might use other good news (positive earnings) to soften the blow of a *reverse stock split* (more on this below).

## NOT ALWAYS TWO FOR ONE

Not all stocks split two for one. Some other frequent ratios for stock splits are three for one, three for two, and five for four. However, regardless of the ratio used, the stock price will decline, and the amount of shares outstanding will increase directly in proportion to the amount of the split. Splits do not give the investor something for nothing in terms of financial gain. Splits do not make a company better or more financially sound.

## WHY DOES THE PRICE RISE?

A price can rise for many reasons, due to pressure from one fact or several factors combined. There are still novice investors who don't realize the price is adjusted to the split. Brokers often hear the confused and complaining phone calls asking what made the price drop so suddenly, especially on a three-for-one split. Though this group is small, it's part of the picture.

Speculators buy either before or soon after an announcement because they believe the price will rise. These short-term traders pick an early exit price at which they will take profits. Their actions account for much of the price weakness that appears shortly after many splits, where they sell. Investors in general still believe the publicity that a stock split is good news for a company. Although the stock does become more affordable for the individual investor, a forward split does nothing to add real value to a company.

## REVERSE STOCK SPLIT

One of the primary reasons for the forward split of a stock is to lower the price. The opposite of a forward split, the purpose of a reverse stock split, is to raise the market price. Companies believe that raising a price will make the stock more attractive for trading. Commonly, reverse splits are one for three, one for 10, or one for 20, but they can be any quantity. In the one-for-10 situation, one share of the new stock is received by the shareholder for every 10 shares owned. Instead of having the original amount of, say, 100 shares, an investor ends up with 10 shares, but the new price is 10 times higher.

Reverse splits are often considered a death knell for a company, but that is not always the case. Some companies reorganize and pull themselves together to become successful. One of the major difficulties is the selling by disappointed investors. Even though the reverse split significantly increases the market price, active selling frequently hammers it back down. To counteract this tendency, companies will sometimes try to time a reverse split announcement to coincide with good news. A positive earnings report, followed by an, "Oh, by the way, we're reverse splitting one for three," can stop some of the shareholders from leaving.

## STOCK SPLIT INVESTING

Over the past 20 years various studies have gone to great lengths to show that forward stock splits are positive events in about 50 percent of the cases. Looking ahead, about half of the companies do well for the following six- and 12-month period. More recently, studies are showing that forward stock splits are positive for good companies. Of course, a strong economy and bull market help. And that is the main problem with any study concerning the effects of a forward stock split: It is impossible to determine how much of the price growth is due to the split, how much is due to growth, and how much is due to a strong market. All of these factors work together to increase the stock's market price.

## BE PRUDENT, BE NEUTRAL

The prudent approach is to treat forward splits as neutral events. If the company is a good investment and the lower price after the split makes it a viable candidate for the portfolio, buy the stock. If a price weakness appears after the stock splits, all the better to save some money.

# CHAPTER 23

# Buy on Weakness,
# Sell on Strength

*Buying on weakness*, when a stock price is declining, should take place carefully and after it has been determined that the company remains fundamentally sound. Many investors have had the unpleasant experience of buying a stock that has dropped in price, only to see it fall further

The price of a good stock in a relatively stable market will tend to move up in surges and then hesitate, sometimes even falling back slightly. It will often drift lower, looking for support from new buyers. When it finds support, the price where buyers enter the market, it will rise again. Investors' taking early profits often cause the hesitation and drifting.

Sometimes this weakness is found in a company that has announced stock buyback programs (and actually does buy back the stock) or has recently increased its dividend. It is usually the stock that had good earnings growth for the same period the previous year. In fact, the earnings probably look good for the preceding three to five years. It is a company that can handle its debt servicing and has a strong balance sheet. It is well managed and one of the growing leaders in its market. The company sticks to the knitting of what it does well, rather than diversifying into unknown areas. It is a company that either is now a dominant force within its own industry or will likely become one.

## NEAR THE TREND LINE

Alberto-Culver came into the new millennium with an attitude toward price growth—a positive attitude. In the time period shown in the chart,

Figure 23-1, any time the price came near the trendline it became a good buy.

Those few times it dropped below the trendline, it became an especially good buy. In March 2000 it was effectively trading at $13.50 a share. In March 2004, the stock rose to $46.00 a share, an increase of $32.50, at least a good triple bagger. Even while the rest of the market was fighting bearish moves, Alberto-Culver went into a consolidation and did not retreat. It had strength and was growing in popularity. Notice the steadily advancing volume of trading.

## MARKET WEAKNESS

Buying on weakness can be looked at as an alternative to using a limit buy order. It's a way to avoid changing the limit order and chasing a price. First analyze and select stock targets. When the market has an off day (not a suspected turn in the trend), check the price quotes on the targets and place an order to buy.

**F I G U R E  23–1**

Alberto-Culver Company, May 1999–March 2004

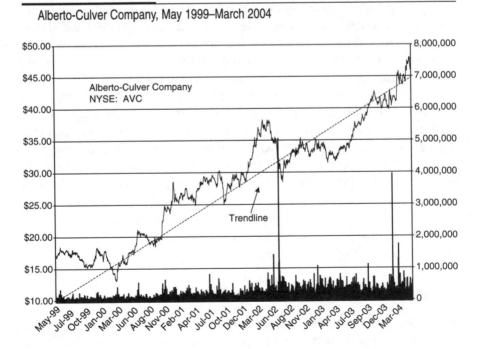

## SELLING ON STRENGTH

Although the investor wants to sell a loser as soon as possible, selling into a rally will obviously produce better results than selling into a price weakness. It can be difficult for many investors to wait for strength. They just want out, immediately, even though a little patience and careful watching could enable them to finesse the sale as the price is rising. Though there will be times when a quick exit is advisable, waiting and selling into strength can often be accomplished.

## A MATTER OF FINESSE

Buying on weakness and selling on strength should be a matter of finesse rather than a total strategy. The finesse enables the investor to be more in control of the situation. It is taking action rather than reacting to a market situation.

At times a strong market will not allow the investor to use finesse. Then it's necessary to take action and buy or sell at the earliest possible moment. But during those times when the investor is in control, finesse can add a few extra dollars to each transaction and make the experience of investing more enjoyable, as well as profitable.

# CHAPTER 24

# It's Better to Average Up Than Down

$P$rice averaging is a prudent strategy with the right stock and situation. There are two ways to lower the average cost of a stock purchase. One is *averaging up* (discussed earlier), and the other is *averaging down* (buying more stock as the price declines). When faced with a dropping share price, when the longer term outlook is believed favorable, it can be worthwhile to hold the current shares and let the price hit bottom. When the price turns and begins to increase, the investor can begin a program of buying at various price levels.

Averaging down, though frequently suggested, is often not the best course of action. It can work in some situations, but it doesn't fit well into most investment plans. Many describe this aggressive strategy as "throwing good money after bad." The problem with averaging down is that it is impossible to know where the price decline will stop.

Implementation of averaging down can also be difficult. Few investors have the discipline to buy more stock at regular intervals as the price continues to drop. The first couple of buys might be acceptable, but continuing to buy becomes more difficult as the price drops lower.

## AVERAGING UP

The results of averaging up can be similar to successful averaging down, but there is less risk involved. Averaging up works as a strategy to enhance the profits of an advancing stock price, and it can work with a stock price in a losing position.

When an investor's stock price suddenly takes a turn for the worse and the price declines significantly due to bad news, the investor holds the position. The investor knows the company and believes the price decline to be a temporary situation. Eventually the stock price will reach a support level and buyers will stop the fall. The investor then plans to average up as the price recovers.

### Bank of America

Take a look at the five-year price action for Bank of America (Figure 24-1). In 1999 and 2000 the price of BAC was in a definite downtrend, primarily being pushed down by the bear market. Early in 2001 the price turned and crossed the downtrend line. An investor who knows and likes the stock sets a strategy to buy 200 shares at the beginning of each quarter.

Notice in Table 24-1 that the average cost per share is significantly less than the last two purchases, made in July and October and signified by italics. Essentially, the investor was buying these shares with a built-in

**F I G U R E   24–1**

Bank of America, January 1999–April 2004

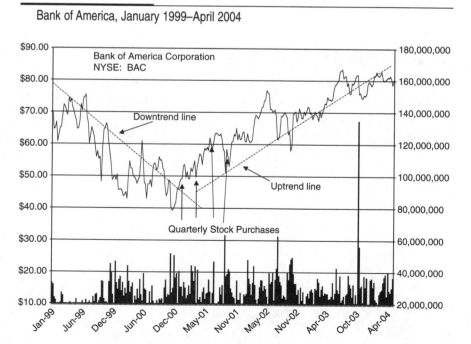

**TABLE 24-1**

Bank of America Stock Purchases, 2001 (Average Up)

| Month | Amount | Price | | Subtotal | Total Investment |
|-------|--------|-------|---|----------|------------------|
| January | 200 shares | $49.00 | = | $9,800 | $9,800 |
| April | 200 shares | 49.59 | = | 9,918 | 19,718 |
| July | 200 shares | 58.36 | = | 11,672 | 29,390 |
| October | 200 shares | 56.13 | = | 11,226 | 0,616 |
| | 800 shares | | | | |
| | $50.77 average cost per share | | | | |

profit. This must be the kind of stock Will Rogers had in mind when he said: "Only buy a stock that the price goes up. If it don't go up, don't buy it."

### Buying at a Discount Continues

As the price of Bank of America continues to rise, so does the discount granted by the averaging up strategy. It's an excellent way to buy stock, and it lowers risk by the amount of that discount.

## BE CAREFUL WITH BUY STOPS

The investor might consider using *buy stop* orders on exchange traded stock, but they should be fully understood and used with caution. The main idea is to buy the stock at regular intervals, thus establishing the "averaging up" strategy.

# CHAPTER 25

# Buy on Monday, Sell on Friday

**P**ublisher and author Yale Hirsch has studied stock market patterns all the way back to 1953. His book *Don't Sell Stocks on Monday* and the annual *Stock Trader's Almanac* have been quite popular with traders and investors. Although Hirsch's statistics are indeed interesting, investors should always keep two points in mind:

- Former performance does not necessarily predict future performance.
- The only certainty is change; if a consistent pattern appears and traders take advantage of it, the pattern changes.

For the 37 years of 1953 to 1989, the market had a tendency to drop on Mondays and rally on Fridays. The saying "Buy on Monday, Sell on Friday" became well-known to those who traded stock. Apparently it became well-known enough for investors to follow the advice.

Starting with 1990, the market pattern of correcting on Mondays ended. In fact, Monday became one of the best days of the week. Obviously, if a majority of investors start buying on Monday, the market will rally.

## STANDARD & POORS 500

Even a recent check of the S&P 500 Index closing levels for 2003 and 2004 no longer show a definite pattern for the buy on Monday, sell on Friday strategy. Of the weeks where both a Monday and a Friday had trading, 28 Fridays closed higher and 18 closed lower. Holiday weekends were not counted. Many of the up Fridays weren't up much. As a trading strategy, it has become more historical than current.

# CHAPTER 26

# Buy Stock Cheaper
# with Dollar Cost Averaging

**W**hat is *dollar cost averaging*? It means to buy stocks with the average cost per share being less than the average share price. This is done by purchasing a larger number of shares when the price of the shares is lower and fewer shares when prices are higher.

## IT'S A DISCIPLINE

Dollar cost averaging is the discipline of setting a regular, long-term investment program for a portfolio, in terms of a set dollar amount that the investor can afford (e.g., $100 or $1,000 invested monthly or quarterly). The periodic investing takes the place of attempting to predict when a stock is at its low or at its high.

By investing the same amount regularly, say, $1,000 every month, the investor will buy more units when prices are low and fewer units when prices are high. The strategy results in a portfolio with an average of costs. Obviously, units purchased at a lower price will outperform those bought at the higher price. Since dollar cost averaging is being used, more of the "high performance units" are bought when prices are low.

### Cisco Systems

Say, for example, an investor wanted to accumulate a position in Cisco Systems. After the proper research, the investor plans to buy on a quarterly basis. The sum of $2,000 will be invested with each purchase. Figure 26-1 shows what would have happened in a 14-month period.

The first $2,000 purchase will buy the stock at $13.71 (145 shares), with a second purchase at $17.50 (114 shares), a third at $20.42 (97 shares), and the forth at $24.00 (83 shares). A total of 439 shares are purchased for about $8,000. The average cost per share is $18.22. On that basis the third and fourth purchases are profitable as soon as purchased. Not a bad way to buy stock.

## AUTOMATIC AND VERSATILE

Dollar cost averaging effectively and automatically cuts back on purchases when the price is high and automatically increases the buys when the price is low. It is a system designed to be used by a long-term investor but just doesn't work well for the short-term trader.

It's versatile as well and can be used with virtually any investment portfolio, although it tends to work better with mutual funds. Funds are

**F I G U R E   26–1**

Cisco Systems, January 2003–March 2004

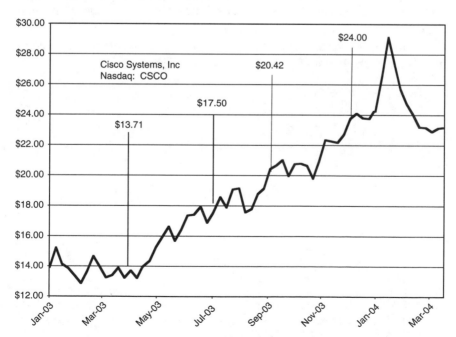

advantageous because their units can be split up, allowing an investor to buy a specific dollar amount instead of a specific number of shares.

Dollar cost averaging also allows one to follow a primary rule of investment: Pay yourself first. Many people don't invest because they believe they don't have enough money to do so. Here again, mutual funds are advantageous because with some funds, investors can put away as little as $50 per month!

## DON'T WORRY ABOUT THE MARKET

The message is that an investor can make good returns even though the market may be unstable. Every investor would like to "buy low and sell high," but that's not an easy thing to do. Markets fluctuate up and down. An investment strategy of dollar cost averaging takes advantage of this variability by consistently investing a fixed amount of money at predetermined intervals (monthly or quarterly). By doing this consistently, the fluctuations in the market value of the investment are smoothed out. The investor using this strategy purchases more shares of stock or a mutual fund when the prices are low and fewer when prices are higher.

Of course, periodic investment plans such as dollar cost averaging do not assure a profit or protect against loss in declining markets. But with the investor using this strategy to continue to make purchases through periods of low and declining prices, he or she gains from purchasing more shares at lower prices. The investor still must carefully select the specific investment, whether stocks, bonds, or mutual funds.

# CHAPTER 27

# The Perfect Hedge
# Is Short Against the Box

Selling short "against the box" means to take a conservative position. It is a position with no loss potential and no gain potential. If an investor owns (long) 100 shares of IBM and sells (short) 100 shares of IBM, the investor's position is short against the box. The strategy is often called the "perfect hedge." If the price of IBM drops, there is no loss. Conversely, if the price rises, there is no gain.

Long 100 IBM at $110 = $11,000

Short 100 IBM at $115 = $11,500

If both positions are closed out, the profit is $500. If the stock price declines, the profit remains $500. If the stock price rises, both positions are closed out and the profit remains at $500.

A short against the box position can be closed by selling the long position and buying back the short position, or by delivering the long shares to close the short. Physically delivering stock to close a short might require a letter of instruction to the broker. No orders are written on delivering, and generally no commission is charged.

The perfect hedge can be useful in a situation in which the investor currently owns the stock but does not have physical possession. This strategy can benefit the investor who is receiving stock from a corporate purchase plan but will not receive the certificate for a few days or weeks. Margin requirements must be fulfilled—Regulation T, which currently requires a deposit of 50 percent, and all margin maintenance calls must be met if the stock continues to rise in price—but the strategy does lock in the price with the short sell. When the investor receives the stock, it can be delivered to close out the short position.

Short selling can be a useful and profitable strategy in the proper situation, but it should be used with caution. The short seller must be aware of the rules and the risks. Obviously, the main risk is the nonparticipation in any future gains. The perfect hedge short sell can be a useful tool in the right situation.

# CHAPTER 28

# Diversification Is the Key to Portfolio Management

If the title of this chapter were correct, virtually any diversified mutual fund of stocks would be the perfect investment. Alas, this is not the case. Although diversification has value as a prudent investment strategy, it also has limitations.

Diversification of investments has been bandied about like some child's favorite rag doll. Actually, it has only a few useful functions and doesn't even begin to offer the amount of protection many people think it does. Many investors place their funds in well-diversified funds, thinking they will be safe from market setbacks. If they watch the price of those funds, they are usually disappointed when the market experiences a severe correction.

Back in the crash of 1987, the disappointment turned to action as many sold out of their declining mutual funds. Their actions became part of the problem creating an even sharper drop in the stock market. As mutual fund investors redeemed (sold) their shares, the fund managers had no choice but to sell into a falling stock market in order to pay out the cash.

## WHAT IS DIVERSIFICATION?

*Portfolio diversification* is the placing of financial assets into significantly different investments in order to increase the chances for large profits, protect against loss, and simplify the analysis and selection process. "Significantly different investments" does not mean buying the shares of three different computer companies. Seagate Technology, Intel, and Apple

Computer might be good computer companies, but investing in these stocks alone would not constitute good diversification. If one invests in a good computer company, a food company, and a department store company, the mix is diversified. Although they are bound by general economic conditions, the diversification is into a growth industry, a defensive industry, and a consumer products industry.

One rationale for diversifying is that having more shots at the profit target enhances the opportunities for profits. It is often difficult to know where the next rapid economic growth will appear. Investing in the stocks of companies in different areas of the economy should increase the chances of participating in surges when they occur. Also, simple logic says the odds of acquiring a winning stock are better when more than one company is selected. When given a chance, most people would rather have 100 chances to win a $1 million than one chance to win $100; the odds are better with more chances.

Safety is also improved when investing in more than one company because the individual problems of one company probably won't affect the others. However, in a bear market or economic recession, diversification won't make much difference unless the diversification extends to companies less affected by economic weaknesses. Just as a declining market influences virtually all stock prices, most companies are impacted by economic slow periods. Companies less affected are those supplying products necessary for basic existence (e.g., food, utilities, and fuel).

## WHAT IF THE MARKET DROPS?

Until the market swings of recent years, many people had assumed diversification also gave them some degree of safety in a market downtrend. In the days leading up to the crash of 1987, market corrections showed mutual fund investors how much their investments could be hurt.

On October 19 many of them started to bail out of their mutual funds, only to see values drop record levels. These mutual fund sellouts were one of the main reasons the Dow Industrial Average fell more than 500 points. Diversification did little to protect investors during this crisis. Sharp corrections that came later did not experience the mutual fund sellouts, suggesting that investors learned something from their first bad experience. A market drop is generally not the best time to sell holdings. If anything, it is a time to look for buying opportunities.

The same was true in the bear market of 2002. As the Nasdaq Composite Index in Figure 28-1 shows, no amount of diversification would have offered any protection. The whole market was dropping

## FIGURE 28–1

Nasdaq Composite Index, January 2002–February 2004

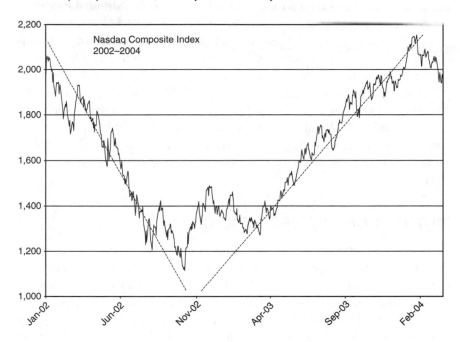

significantly. Being in a money market would have saved some of the loss from happening, but staying in the market and riding out the storm would also have helped. Keep in mind that the Standard & Poor's 500 Index and the Dow Industrial Average had a similar track for 2002.

## HOW MUCH DIVERSIFICATION IS ENOUGH?

How much diversification depends on the experience, time for analysis, and assets available to the investor. Investment advisers can give glib answers: "If you have $10,000 to invest, it should be diversified in 10 companies and three different industries." But this won't work well. Even buying round lots of 100 shares as low as $25 would enable an investor to buy the stocks of only four companies, and this would mean adding extra money for fees or commissions.

The 10-company rule would create several odd lots of stock. There is no depth to such investing. Remember the axiom from Chapter 20: "Make Winners Win Big." It would be better to avoid the odd lot situation (less than 100 shares) and begin with diversification into three or four different stocks in three industries. This will still provide safety, and increase the chances of selecting a good winner. Later on either the depth or the breadth of diversification can be increased with additional money to invest.

Also, think of the time involved in analyzing and selecting 10 companies. How about the amount of time required to maintain a close watch on the performance of those 10 companies in three industries? Most people will allocate some time for stock portfolio, market, and economic analysis, but the last thing they want is for it to become a second job.

It should also be noted that too much diversification can dilute performance significantly. In some circumstances an investor would probably be better off in U.S. Treasury securities or insured certificates of deposit (CDs).

## MUTUAL FUND DIVERSIFICATION

A growing number of investment articles are now appearing regarding diversification with mutual funds. How many mutual funds are enough? Since mutual funds are already diversified, how much more diversification is necessary? Some articles will say no more than 10 mutual funds, others no more than five. Several advisers go the intellectual route and say one mutual fund in each asset class. At least one adviser is said to base the decision on how much paperwork an investor can tolerate.

Dilution enters into this as well. It's possible that owning too many mutual funds may position an investor at a point of diminishing returns.

## ARE THERE OTHER WAYS TO DIVERSIFY?

A practical diversification strategy that will protect all of the original capital is to buy U.S. Treasury bonds and use the interest from them to invest in the stock market. If the bonds are held to maturity, the principal is never at risk. Instead it is returned as the bonds reach maturity.

Another form of easy diversification is to take half of the money available for investment and buy zero coupon U.S. Treasury securities with a maturity date out far enough to double in value. If the entire stock portfolio goes to zero (which is unlikely, unless highly speculative companies are selected), the investor will retain the principal when the bonds mature. Obviously, there is a high opportunity cost if this unlikely event occurs. Although both of these approaches have tax implications and some risk, they are valid strategies for investing with lower risk.

## IT IS IMPORTANT

Diversification is important in an investment strategy. It can be used to lower the overall risk and increase the chances for better profits. It's important to remember that risk is not eliminated because of diversification. All investing carries some risk; therefore, it is prudent for the investor to be aware of strategies to moderate that danger. This said, diversification of the investment portfolio can be an excellent risk-moderating strategy.

# PART IV

# Trading

In many ways, this entire book is about trading. Not "day trading," which can be a course to overtrading disaster for many investors, but rather the long-term trading that might be practiced in your retirement account.

It used to be said that the only time to sell a stock is when you have found a new one to buy. With the extended bull market of the past decade, this has changed to something like the only time to sell a stock is when you believe it cannot live up to your growth expectations. If the stocks are researched well before they are bought, most of the trading here will be buying rather than selling.

Why is it best to trade "at the market" (Chapter 30)? You might also ask why risk your entire trading strategy for a few extra cents per share? When the market moves, it moves. It doesn't sit there and wait to execute every limit order.

Why not buy a stock because it has a low price (Chapter 31)? Because there is a reason it has a low price, and the reason is very often an exact reason not to buy the stock at all. This one trips up many beginning investors who believe that if they pay fewer dollars, they're not taking much risk. Frankly, the risk couldn't be much higher, but the stock price can—and usually does—go lower.

# CHAPTER 29

# Never Short a Dull Market

**A** *dull market* is a *sideways market*, sometimes also referred to as a *trendless market*. Movement is slow, with an occasional advance followed by a small correction. During dull or balanced markets, institutional investors are all waiting (if they can) for a good reason to get back into the market. The slightest good news (or sometimes bad news that is not as bad as expected) can cause a strong rally to develop. The rally can cause the price of the short stock to rise sharply, resulting in margin calls and eventually a loss. The proof of market strength is shown by the stability creating the dullness. If there were no underlying strength, the market would obviously be falling.

All lethargic markets have occasional rallies and corrections, although the price swings are generally not severe. If an investor can identify where the heaviest volume occurs, it is possible to determine whether the sentiment is bullish or bearish. If the volume on a correction (downward movement) is consistently and significantly greater than the volume on a rally, the sentiment trends to be bearish.

During the year after the crash of 1987, investors were overly cautions (Figure 29-1). Much of 1988 had a dull, lethargic market that tended to have heavier volume on rallies and lighter volume on corrections. Most of the rally action was caused by *dividend capture*, which is the buying of a stock just for the purpose of receiving the dividend.

Looking at the Dow Industrials for that 10-year period, we can see various dull markets. Only the 1989 through 1990 market had a sharp drop

## FIGURE 29-1

Dow Industrial Averages, 1987–1998

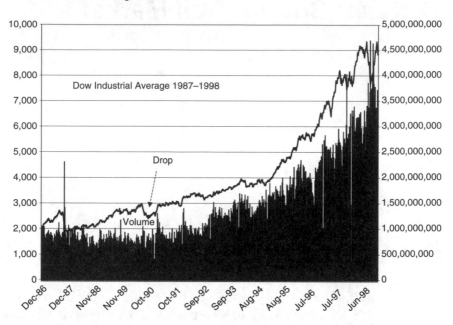

at the end of the dullness, and even that was followed by a resumption of the uptrend. Other years show corrections, but they do not show a change in trend. After a short-lived correction, they resume the uptrend. Short sellers covering their short positions usually start rallies at the end of these brief corrections.

A more recent dull market in 2002, depicted in the Nasdaq monthly chart in Figure 29-2, showed the market holding position. There were two downtrends, but the uptrend continued at the end of the year. A few areas offered short selling opportunities, but they followed a downward penetration of the short-term uptrend. The opportunities were small and over quickly. They would have been difficult to trade on the short side.

The market goes flat, nothing much going on, and the investor gets an urge to sell short. Before doing so it is usually a good idea to look very closely at the stock market and the stock selection for the short sale. Dull markets often have underlying strength keeping them stable. Buyers step in to replace sellers and the market becomes trendless. A short sale in the dull market shown on the monthly chart could have ended quite painfully. Look at the Nasdaq daily chart in Figure 29-3 to see what happened next.

### FIGURE 29–2

Nasdaq Composite Index (Monthly), September 2002–March 2003

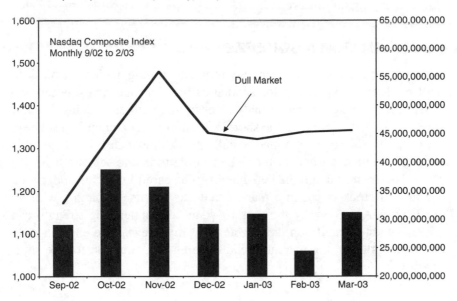

### FIGURE 29–3

Nasdaq Composite Index (Daily), September 2002–March 2004

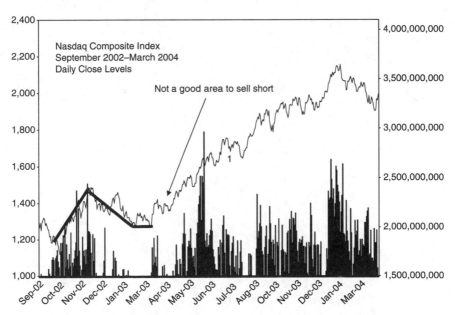

The daily chart makes it immediately clear how unwise a short sell would have been. The Nasdaq Composite Index went from being nearly flat to a roaring bull market.

## LOOK OUT FOR A SQUEEZE

Selling short is a speculative strategy requiring timing, patience, and skill. Dull markets are notorious for sudden rallies that put the "squeeze" on short sellers. In fact, traders usually refer to these rallies as being a "short squeeze" or "squeezing out the shorts." A short seller caught in a squeeze runs the risk of receiving a margin call for additional cash or marginable securities to be deposited, or the risk of being forced to sell at a loss.

"Never short a dull market" means to be careful with the underlying strength of stock prices in a market that has become lethargic, with no clear trend. As shown by the past 10 years, the underlying strength can turn to buying activity on the slightest positive news. The ensuing rally and resumption of the uptrend creates a high-risk situation for the short investor.

# CHAPTER 30

# It's Best to Trade at the Market

**M**arket orders have priority. It's important to remember that fact. A market order says that the investor is willing to buy or sell shares immediately at the "best available price." The order takes precedence over any other kind of order. It must be presented to the "trading crowd" by the specialist on the stock exchange, at the earliest possible moment. In reality, a computer matches the vast majority of market orders. The result is a nearly immediate execution and report.

## IMPLICATIONS OF A MARKET ORDER

A market order implies that the investor desires a fast execution. It says that the investor wants to buy or sell the stock immediately. The only time delay that occurs is when a broker is entering the order.

It also implies that any price is acceptable. That fact is often forgotten until an investor pays more than expected for a stock purchase or receives less than anticipated on a sell. In a steady, evenly paced market, a buy order will be filled at or near the current offer on the stock quote, and at or near the bid on a sell.

In a fast-market situation, an investor could pay a few or even several dollars more per share when his or her order is actually executed. This can be of real concern in a takeover situation, where $20 or $60 or more extra per share might be paid with a market order. It is the main reason takeover offers are normally not announced during trading hours. The uncertainty of price necessitates that buyers check the current trading price when placing an order to buy or sell stock.

Although the vast majority of trades are filled at one price, a market order is quoted in terms of a *round lot*, normally 100 shares, although there are exceptions. This practice may create a problem with thinly traded stocks. If necessary, multiple round lots can be broken into smaller lots, with different prices.

## LIMIT ORDER CONTRADICTS DESIRE TO SELL

The main reason it's best to trade at the market is simply that the market moves quickly. Order qualifiers such as price limits or *all or none* (AON) do not have the same priority as market orders and might not be filled. Directions can quickly and unexpectedly change, leaving the investor twisting in the wind with a limit order. When a decision has been reached, why should an investor take an action directly contradicting the strategy? I want to buy some stock because I believe the price will rise, but I might be able to get it cheaper. So I place an order below the current price. Why do such a thing? Why buy a stock believing the price will go lower? On the other hand, why sell a stock believing it will rise higher in price? The actions don't match the strategies.

The idea of placing a buy or sell of securities as a market order is to obtain an immediate execution at the best available price. If the investor nitpicks over a few cents per share, opportunity is lost, and the ensuing cost of frustration and time lost is high. Such costs can easily be higher than any movement in the stock price while the market order is being placed. Do the analysis, make the decision, set the strategy, and stick with it when placing the order.

The only time to avoid using a market order is when a price is rising rapidly. If an investor is interested in a company whose stock price is rapidly moving up, but the investor desires to have some control over the buying price, a limit order or better can be entered. The term "or better" is normally assumed, but in this situation its intent is to confirm that a limit order is being placed above the current trading price.

Let's say that XYZ Corp. is currently trading at $50 a share, up $5 for the day. An investor wants to buy the stock but wants some control over price. An order to buy 100 shares is placed with a limit of 50¼ or better for the day. Since the limit is above the market price, it might be considered an error if the "or better" qualifier is not added. At this point either the order will be filled between 50 to 50¼ or it will not be executed.

Although this can be a good strategy on the buy side, on the sell side it is different. Although a similar order can be placed on the sell side, it might not be prudent. If the price is dropping rapidly and a decision has been made to sell, it should be sold as quickly as possible. There is a risk that placing a limit on the sell order will result in the order not being executed.

## BEST AVAILABLE PRICE

*Market order* means to buy or sell stock at the "best available price." If an order is filled at a price considerably away from the quote given to the investor, the time of sales can be checked with the broker to see why the order was executed at the price reported. Although errors are possible, they are usually the exception.

Another instance in which it might not be advisable to use a market order is with low-priced, usually thinly traded stock—for example, speculative stock that sells for less than $10 a share. In these situations a limit order is usually best, but again there is still the risk that it won't be executed.

## FAIR AND ORDERLY MARKET

Exchanges and over-the-counter market makers strive to fill orders quickly and as close to the current price as possible. It's part of the integrity essential to maintaining a fair and orderly market. If a public market for securities does not operate with this integrity, it will cease to exist as a continuous public auction. Stock exchanges around the world, whether in emerging or developed markets, are striving to make their markets fair, orderly, and stable. Many have adopted rules to stop trading if a stock's price or the market fluctuates beyond a certain percentage in a trading session. Calling a halt to the trading won't stop declines, but it will allow everyone an opportunity to learn about the situation.

In most situations market orders work best, because they can be executed rapidly at a reasonable fill price. Most of the time these advantages outweigh the benefits of placing a limit order, which often cannot be executed. If bad fills are being received, they should be checked for possible errors and the strategy should be reexamined.

# CHAPTER 31

# Never Buy a Stock Because It Has a Low Price

Buying a stock just because it has a low price is often a risky strategy. It's especially risky if the investor doesn't find out why the price is so low. Often, investors are attracted to low-priced stocks that pay a dividend. The lower price pushes the dividend percent higher. The yield on the dividend might be 10, 15, 20 percent, or higher. Sometimes the companies that own the stocks are about to severely reduce or even eliminate the dividend. When they do so, the stock price plummets even further. The investor is then left with an extremely low-priced stock and no dividend.

## HOW CAN A STOCK BE OVERSOLD?

A stock is *oversold* when selling drives its price below its value. The then undervalued stock is expected to show some kind of rally in the next few trading sessions. Some analysts and investors don't believe an "oversold" situation can actually exist because the term implies that investors sold more shares than they intended to sell. Actually, the term "oversold" refers to the price at which a significant number of buyers come to the stock, believing it is worth more than the current market price reflects. It can be accompanied by higher trading volume.

On the other end, *overbought* is the price at which volume decreases and investors start selling because they believe the current market price is too high.

Technical analysts frequently use these two terms. Fundamental analysts might use *overvalued* or *undervalued*. They would tend to look at the price in relation to earnings and revenues.

## PepsiCo

In situations where the price drops, buyers enter the scene and force the price back up, overselling the stock. This can be an ideal time to buy a stock, if you're aware of the full situation. PepsiCo's price, shown in Figure 31-1, tends to drop and rise on a regular basis, providing excellent opportunities to save a few dollars on a stock purchase.

Two facts are important: (1) The price recovers from these oversold conditions and (2) the basic fundamentals of PepsiCo's business remain sound.

## Enron

As Enron hit the skids, it was a long and fast ride from a high of more than $87 a share to zero (Figure 31-2). This is an obvious example for *not* buying because it had a low price. The price was on its way to the bottom and not likely to recover anytime soon. Although there can be a case for buying stocks in a "turnaround" situation, it's usually not a good strategy if the company has gone into bankruptcy.

## F I G U R E   31–1

PepsiCo, April 2000–March 2004

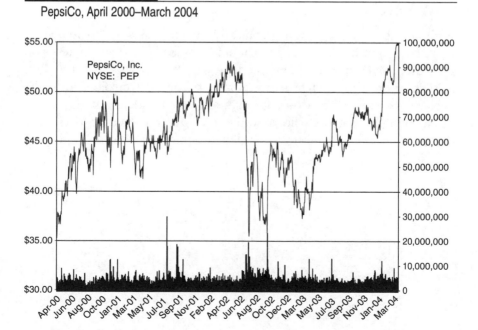

**F I G U R E   31–2**

Enron Corporation, April 1999–April 2004

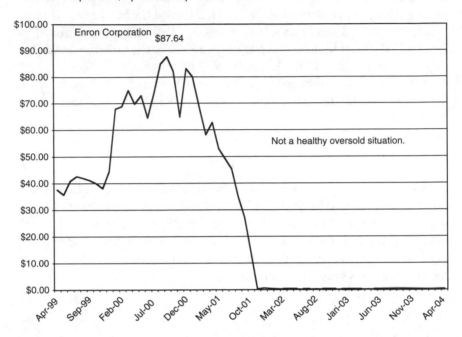

## LOW PRICE

Apropos the Enron situation graphically depicted above, "Never buy a stock because it has a low price" should be amended to say, "unless you are reasonably certain of when the price will recover and how it will do so." There are times when a stock price becomes oversold due to the impact of bad news. The oversold condition can provide an excellent buying opportunity for those who know the stock. It might be time to add new shares to an existing portfolio or obtain a new investment at bargain prices.

# CHAPTER 32

# Buy the Dips

Stock prices tend to move as a group, which causes the stock market to fluctuate. The market virtually never moves in a straight line. The stock market moves as anticipation changes, based on reactions to economic developments. Although in 1929 the market stayed down for four years, and in 1977 it stayed down five years, most market declines are more short term. Many last only four to six months:

> For 10 straight years, every time the stock market has taken a hit, you've made big money if you jumped in with both feet. A "buy the dips" philosophy has outperformed any other strategy imaginable.

James Cramer, who has been a renowned hedge fund manager on Wall Street, goes on to say how the one exception to this was the market crash of 1987. But the biggest difference between then and the 1990s is the fact that interest rates were rising in 1987.

Notice that Mr. Cramer talks about the "stock market" taking a hit, not the individual stock. Dips caused by market declines are usually the most profitable; however, individual companies can have temporary setbacks that are resolved and the price recovers and climbs to new highs. When the dip is caused by market pressure, the reason why isn't so important. When the dip is just the individual stock, the reason why becomes extremely important. Find out why the stock price is down and what needs to happen for it to recover.

## DIPS ON MARKET PRESSURE

A look at the price of Federated Department Stores in Figure 32-1 shows some excellent buying on the dip opportunities.

Obviously, the price dips of November 2000 and December 2001 were mostly due to market pressure. However, the most recent price dip, in February 2003, was not caused by a declining market. Sales were off and the company went through some strategic realignment, a situation worthy of further study. Buying any one of the three dips would have resulted in virtually a 100 percent gain. That can be simple market timing, which pays off handsomely.

## SELLING ON THE RALLIES

Buying on the dips can be used by the short-term speculator or the long-term investor. Some speculators follow a strategy of buying on the dips and selling on the rallies. Obviously, the ideal stock for this trading is one that tends to fluctuate on a regular basis

### F I G U R E   32–1

Federated Department Stores and Dow Industrial Average, April 1999–April 2004

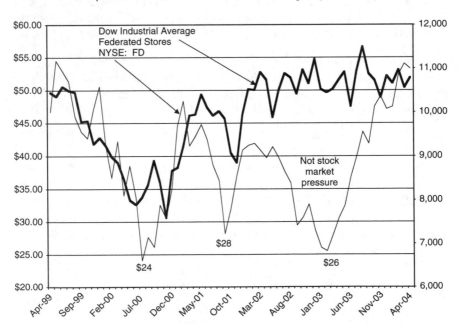

## BUY STOP STRATEGY

All of the dips shown in Federated's price are caused primarily by market corrections. As we said, a speculator buying on these dips could have profited nearly 100 percent. The major difficulty with such a strategy is knowing when to make the move. A possible strategy, once the price drops, would be to place a buy stop order (on exchange-traded stock) above the current price. That way the buy wouldn't be made until the stock moved upward. The stop could be lowered if the price continued to drop. A limit placed on the buy stop could give protection from an extreme upsurge.

The dips here could also be good for long-term investors. Price weakness, caused primarily by market weakness, can provide excellent opportunities to add stocks to a portfolio position.

## IT'S A NO-BRAINER

To buy stock on price dips is a sound strategy, especially when those dips are caused by stock market corrections. Certainly, the stock market might keep correcting and enter a bear market, but this is not what usually happens. Most corrections stop quickly and the market recovers. Individual stock prices that are influenced by the market create buying opportunities for both the speculator and the long-term investor. These opportunities do not usually last for a long period; therefore, the investor should have targets analyzed and selected in advance to move swiftly.

# CHAPTER 33

# Order Modifications Might Cause Delay

**C**areful consideration should be given to any modification placed on an order, because an order with any qualifiers other than *market order* can take more time to be executed.

## GOOD TILL CANCELED (GTC)

The order stays "open" until it is executed, canceled, or changed by the investor, or until it is canceled by the brokerage firm. Brokerage firms have different policies as to how long they will carry an open order on their books. Many cancel at the end of 30 days or the end of the following month, whereupon the order must be reentered to remain open. Automatic cancellation helps the investor remember the open order and prevents duplications.

Open orders can be changed or canceled by the investor at any time; however, the investor should question the value of making several changes, usually referred to as *chasing*. It's usually better to make the trade than it is to chase a price. Changes are costly to the brokerage firms, and those costs end up being passed on to investors. Also, too many changes can lead to confusion and costly errors.

## DO NOT REDUCE (DNR)

Buy and stop GTC orders are generally modified by the instruction *DNR*, which simply means "do not reduce." Most investors want an order filled even if it has become *ex-dividend*, which means the investor is buying the stock without the current dividend attached. The stock's price is reduced by the amount of the dividend at the beginning of trading. Many firms require the DNR designation on all GTC orders.

When an investor decides to change an open order, it is necessary to notify the broker of the existing, previously placed order. Otherwise, two orders could be executed, with the investor bearing responsibility for any liabilities. A new or changed GTC order does not automatically cancel a previously entered order.

The advantage of the good-till-canceled order is its automatic feature. The order stays in effect, day after day, and it does not need to be reentered until it is changed or canceled. The investor's transaction will be executed when it is possible to do so, and it does not need constant attention. The disadvantage of using an open order is that doing so could cause delay. Situations may arise where other limit orders have been placed at the same price. The investor's order execution is delayed by "stock ahead." Also, keep in mind that market orders always take precedence.

Market orders are automatically "day orders," but they may be entered GTC on thinly traded stocks. Some preferred stock and issues from small companies are not traded every day.

## DAY ORDER

The *day order* is just what it says: It's an order placed for the day only. If the order cannot be executed by the end of the trading session, it is canceled. A notice of the cancellation is sent to the broker: "firm nothing done." The broker notifies the investor. A day order can be changed or canceled by the investor at any time during the trading session.

The frequent trader or day trader is likely to use day orders. Their strategy is normally based on momentum that is building during the day, so they have no reason to keep an order open longer than the current trading session. The main disadvantage of using the day order is that the investor must wait for a status report at the end of the trading session. Obviously, the report can take longer after an exciting day in the stock market.

## OB: OR BETTER

The phrase "or better" refers to the price most advantageous to the investor. "Or better" is always assumed with limit buy orders placed below, or sell orders placed above, the current trading price. Usually the OB designation is added to a buy limit placed at or above the current price, and on sell orders at or below the current price. The OB designation clarifies the investor's intent to buy or sell.

For example, let's say that the stock of ABX is trading at 21¼ and is up 1¼ from the previous day's closing price of $20 a share. The full quote is shown in Table 33-1:

The investor wishes to buy ABX and take advantage of a continuing uptrend; however, a market order could fill higher than the current ask price. This might present an extra problem in an IRA account that is limited to the funds available. The investor is willing to pay as much as 21½, but only if necessary. The OB also confirms that the investor is serious and that the order is not an error. Since limit buy orders are usually placed below the current price, a limit placed above might be considered an error and be returned for clarification.

The order is entered as a limit, or better: "Buy 500 shares ABX at a limit of 21½ or better, day order." If the order can be executed, the investor will buy the 500 shares for 21½ a share or less. If the price is higher than the limit by the time the order is entered and stays higher, the order will be canceled at the end of the day.

The advantage of using "or better" with a limit is price control. The obvious disadvantage is that the order might not be executed.

## AON: ALL OR NONE

The qualifier *all or none* can be used with multiple round lot or block orders. Block orders normally receive special handling through a brokerage firm's block order desk. The purpose of the modifier is to avoid a partial fill of an order.

If a person desires to buy 1,000 shares of BBB Corporation at $20 a share, with the stock currently at 19⅞ to 21⅛, a limit order can be entered at $20 or better for the day. It might be possible to buy only 500 or 600 shares at that price. The order can be filled for 500 shares at $20 a share,

**T A B L E  33-1**

Bid Details

| Symbol | Last | Change | Bid | Ask |
|--------|------|--------|-----|-----|
| ABX | 21¼ | + 1¼ | 21 | 21¼ |

leaving the investor 500 shares short. If the AON modifier is added, there are only two possibilities at the end of the trading session: Either the investor will have bought 1,000 shares of BBB at $20 a share or the order will have been canceled because it could not be filled.

Even though a partial fill might be desirable in some stock situations, in most cases the investor would rather have the total amount of shares. If limit orders are entered "good till canceled," a separate, full commission could be charged for each day a partial fill occurs, thereby increasing the investor's cost.

The main advantage to the all-or-none modifier is that it enables the investor to control the filled quantity. It must all be executed at the same time and price. The major disadvantage is that in some situations the order will be difficult to fill.

## IMMEDIATE OR CANCEL (IOC)

The IOC order modifier is added to a limit that is at or close to an executable price. It specifies a maximum quantity, but it can be less. It says to buy (sell) 2,000 shares right now if you can. If you cannot, buy (sell) 1,500 or 1,000 shares and cancel the remainder of the order.

## FILL OR KILL (FOK)

Although similar to the IOC, the FOK says to make the transaction for the full amount immediately or cancel the order. This differs from the AON, which allows some time to fill the order at the limit price.

## NOT HELD (NH)

Used primarily with large orders, the NH modification allows the floor broker to use time or price discretion for the effective execution of an order. *Not held* indicates that the investor will accept what the floor broker can accomplish with the execution of the trade.

Note: During unusually fast markets, brokerage firms may accept only "market orders not held," meaning they are not held to a price based on the current price quotation. When the system becomes overloaded, orders ahead can change the price showing on the computer by the time an investor's order is cleared.

## ODD LOT ON SALE

Occasions can arise when an investor is selling a combination of a round lot (usually 100 shares) and an odd lot (less than the round lot) of stock.

An amount such as 125 shares of XYZ Company is a combination of the round lot of 100 and the odd lot of 25 shares.

If a limit order is placed to sell the stock, the investor might want to add the modification *odd lot on sale* to indicate that the round lot is available at the limit price, but the odd lot may be sold at the market price. This modifier simplifies the transaction and makes it easier to have the order executed. The odd lot portion of 25 shares could be charged an extra one-eighth of a dollar (12½ cents). The extra fee is known as the *odd lot differential,* and it is assessed for the extra costs involved with trading an odd lot of stock.

Placing a combination round lot/odd lot sell order with the odd-lot-on-sale modifier can make execution of the trade easier and faster. The only disadvantage is that the investor must accept a lower price for the odd lot shares.

Modifiers such as price limits, AON, or IOK, can have an impact on the speed at which an order is executed. Although there can be sound reasons for placing limits and other modifiers on buy and sell orders, in most cases the time saved by placing a market order is worth more than the time lost waiting for another 12½ cents per share. Placing market orders will usually save the investor time and money.

# CHAPTER 34

# Avoid Overtrading

**F**or some people, the trading of stocks, options, or other securities can become an addiction similar to gambling. It can be like a nickel or dime stock machine: Win a few jackpots and keep putting the coins back in until they are gone. It's like betting on one more horse to make up for the losses or to extend the winnings.

As with other gambling addictions, trading-addicted people are usually not making any money. At best they tend to break even, which only adds to their compulsive activity. The day is just not complete unless they can make one or two stock or option trades.

## ADDICTION AND COMPLIANCE

Every brokerage firm has a few stories of a stock or option trader who became addicted to trading. The stories usually involve fairly large sums of money after a few years' time. Eventually, the trading-addicted investor runs out of money or the brokerage firm's compliance department steps in and puts a halt to the activity. Compliance departments are quite diligent in this regard, although it is difficult for them to watch every account closely.

One such story involves an investor who became addicted to trading index options on the Standard & Poor's 100 Index, often referred to as the OEX Index. During a three-year period, this investor traded an average of two to five times each day. He consistently lost an average of $10,000 every year. When the compliance department brought the activity to a halt, the customer's biggest disappointment was not the money lost, but rather, being forced to close the account because the $2,000 minimum equity in a margin account could not be maintained.

The investor did have a disciplined approach to trading. Sometimes the strategy worked, and other times it failed to produce anything but losses. The system was possibly too inflexible to deal with the daily changes in the stock market, although it was not helped by a compulsive need to make a trade every day. The investor was continually warned (by the brokerage firm's compliance department) about the risk, losses, and speculative nature of his trading strategy.

The main failing of the compulsive system seemed to be the missed opportunities caused by closing out the option positions too soon. In several situations the investor had the right idea but did not allow time for the strategy to do its work. If the investor had waited patiently only a couple of days, the positions would have been profitable.

## OVERTRADING AND CHURNING

The securities industry regulatory organizations consider overtrading and *churning* to be nearly the same activity. Most people think of churning as a stockbroker-initiated activity, but the end result is the same. The activity generates commission charges for the stockbroker and the brokerage firm. Unsuitable trading, where recommendations are not in keeping with the customer's financial condition, investing sophistication, or investment objectives, is a related activity.

For overtrading to constitute churning, the broker must exercise control over the trading in the account and abuse the customer's trust by engaging in transactions that are excessive in volume and frequency, considering the character of the account.

## UNSUITABLE TRADING

The NASD suitability rule requires that the broker's recommendations be appropriate in light of the customer's financial condition, level of sophistication, investment objectives, and risk tolerance. The suitability rule and the closely related "know your customer" rule (NYSE Rule 405) require that the broker use due diligence to obtain information about the customer's financial situation, needs, objectives, and understanding.

Violation of NASD and stock exchange rules, including the suitability and know-your-customer rules, may be the basis for a cause of action on its own. For example, the violation of the suitability rule and the NASD rules may itself constitute a basis for a breach-of-contract action.

Unsuitable trading has also been held to constitute fraud and a violation of federal and state securities laws. A broker clearly is prohibited from recommending unsuitable investments, and there have been indications that a broker should refuse to execute unsuitable transactions even when the investment is originally the customer's idea.

## PREVENTING OVERTRADING

Overtrading can be difficult to control, especially with increasing access to the market through the Internet. The flexibility, convenience, and accessibility of information can encourage the investor to trade more frequently. When working with a brokerage firm, carefully checking records can help the investor prevent overtrading. Taking the time to analyze the trades on a monthly statement can help the investor stay in control of the amount of trading. Other ideas are presented below.

### Keep Organized Records

Look carefully at the monthly statement from the brokerage firm, and make a short note as to the reason for each trade. If you normally do a lot of trading in a month, you should keep these notes on the confirmation slips that arrive by mail a few days after the transaction.

Ideally, you should keep notes on your strategy in a stock trading log. That way, you are making the notation at the time of the transaction, when the strategy is still fresh in your mind. The notation should briefly mention how the trade fit into the specific strategy and possibly the overall plan you have prepared.

### Look for Profit in Transactions

Although an account can be profitable but still overtraded, it's worse to be losing and overtraded. If there have been several unprofitable transactions, it's time to reassess or redefine your objectives or strategy. In this situation, checking the timing of the trades can be helpful. Might the delay of a week or two have increased the profits? Perhaps you should check your analysis of the current market strength.

### Look for Patterns in Trading

Are trades occurring every day or every other day? Is there a pattern such as trading every three out of five days on a consistent basis? If you notice a pattern, what is the cause of it? Finding a pattern might point out trading that is becoming or has become an addiction.

## Assess Your Contact with the Broker

Is this contact on a daily basis, or is it several times a day, perhaps even hourly? Very close contact with the market can easily lead an investor to overtrade an account. The individual can develop an addiction to the market action. The information addiction can easily cause the investor to overreact to minor moves in the stock market. The first overreaction leads to another, and soon the account is in an overtraded tailspin.

Overtrading and trading addiction can be detrimental to any investment strategy. It is extremely difficult to build profits when too many transactions are being whipsawed by short-term market swings. Flexible strategies, good records, solid investment objectives, and pulling away from unprofitable market activity can help an investor avoid many of the pitfalls.

# P A R T   V

# Good Ideas

"It is easier to follow a few stocks well than it is to follow a well full of stocks." This statement was made by S. A. Nelson, more than 100 years ago. He was a close friend of Charles Dow, the founding father of Dow Jones & Company. Many investors are guilty of trying to follow too many stocks, so many that they can't keep their facts straight. How many to follow is always an arbitrary decision, but if a person follows the stocks he or she currently owns and maybe as many as five others, that should be plenty. If an investor owns stock of five companies and follows five others, 10 stocks are more than enough to follow and try to remember.

Several investment advisers are guilty of recommending too many stocks in which to diversify or to follow. Possibly, this is intended to make the investor dependent on the adviser's expertise. An investor wants to invest and make a certain return, but usually doesn't want the effort to become a second job.

This part also explores other good ideas in investing, things that should be remembered, like "Never Get Married to a Stock." As obvious as this statement is, it's amazing how many people will hang on to hope for a stock until the company shuts its doors forever.

Keeping good records is an obvious advantage, and investing in what you know best is one of those simple rules that people often either don't think of or forget outright.

# CHAPTER 35

# Follow a Few Stocks Well

$F$ollowing stocks can be interesting and exciting, or it can be tedious and frustrating. To many investors it is the information that starts their day. They thrill to poring over the *Wall Street Journal* or *Barron's* or *Investor's Business Daily* and other financial journals. Others spend a great deal of time "surfing the net" to find out what happened in the stock market and then learn everyone's opinion of why it happened. Some of these fastidious readers seldom invest in the stock market; they just enjoy the changes, like watching a World Series or perhaps the Super Bowl. They are the armchair investors who get enjoyment from seeing how the game plays out. For others—real investors—watching the market is not nearly as exciting as participating in its gains.

## LEARNING THE BASIC SKILLS

To become skilled in stock watching or tracking, one must have first-hand experience. An investor will learn more by owning a stock for two weeks than by watching a stock for two years. The reason is simple: Ownership places money at risk. Risk of losing money greatly heightens one's attention. Losses that occur when the price drops are real losses. More important, gains that occur when the price rises are potential profits; thus the company and its price progress become a magnet to the investor's attention.

During the first few days of ownership, an investor is likely to learn more about the company than he or she will for the rest of the holding

period. Keeping some of this enthusiasm can prove useful in making
sound investment decisions.

## THREE INFLUENCES ON STOCK PRICES

The price of a stock has essentially three main influences:

- Direction and strength of the overall stock market
- The current "play," or investing theme
- Earnings

### Direction and Strength

At times, the direction and strength of the stock market are difficult to determine. However, reading opinions from newspapers, magazines, and other
periodicals can provide considerable information on strength and direction.

### Where's the Play?

The "play," or theme, is usually found in the industry group or sector, such
as technology, computers, the Internet, oil, health care, waste management, etc. In some industries the play can be illusive, such as in fiberop-
tics, drug rehabilitation, or lasers. The potential of lasers has excited people for more than 30 years, and yet few companies have accomplished
much as "laser companies."

Play can be further complicated by a company's diversification into
other industries, such as tobacco companies moving into food products.

Classifying stocks by theme, or play (merger, bad news, legal action,
and others), helps to focus attention on what happens with the group.
When the news headline says, STOCKS WERE UP TODAY ON WALL STREET,
FUELED BY STRENGTH IN THE COMPUTER TECHNOLOGY GROUP, the computer
investor's attention is drawn to the information. If OPEC members are
fighting among themselves and producing too much oil, the prices of oil
stocks drop. However, if oil-producing countries are in a cooperative
mood, prices remain stable (or increase), oil company earnings increase,
and the stock prices usually rise accordingly.

### Anticipate Earnings

The trick is to trade on the anticipation of earnings rather than on the specific earnings increase. Once the earnings increase (sometimes an earnings surprise) is announced, the price moves up immediately. Many

investors buying at this point are actually buying the stock at inflated prices. When the reality of this becomes apparent, the price retreats. A small profit can quickly become a disappointing temporary loss.

## Positive Earnings for Sysco Corp.

In January of 2004, Standard & Poor's gave a positive earnings announcement and buy recommendation on Sysco Corporation, an institutional food service company:

> Sysco (SYY ): Reiterates 5 STARS (buy)
>
> The hospitality-services company posted earnings per share of 34 cents, vs. 28 cents—2 cents above S&P's estimate. Sales grew 10.8%, on 2.7% real growth, 7.3% food-cost inflation, and 0.8% from acquisitions. Sysco continues to focus on eliminating its less profitable customer accounts while expanding its reach through acquisitions and internal growth. S&P is raising its fiscal 2004 (June) earnings per share estimate by 3 cents, to $1.41, on an expectation of benefits from lower food-cost inflation, higher sales of private-label goods, and acquisition and technology efficiencies. S&P is raising the 12-month target price by $2, to $45, based on *discounted cash-flow* and *price-earnings* analyses.
>
> *(Joseph Agnese, "S&P Buy Sysco,"*
> BusinessWeek Online, *January 6, 2004)*

## Trend Resumed

The price of Sysco responded favorably to the earnings surprise. It then encountered other stock market problems that forced the price lower. After three fairly strong attempts to reach new highs and continue the uptrend, the price of Sysco turned and penetrated the uptrend line. Volume tended to be stronger on price rises than on declines.

Where the price of Sysco goes from this point depends on the anticipation of whether the company can sustain earnings performance. The impact of earnings tends to be a long-term influence unless something else negative occurs.

## Earnings Surprises Can Be Negative

Just as a positive earnings surprise can push a price higher, a negative earnings surprise, coming in below expectations, can force a price lower. As stated, negative earnings surprises can even outweigh positive economic indicators:

> Poor earnings reports from several companies late Thursday, including Sun Microsystems Inc. and DoubleClick Inc., weighed down technology shares in Friday trading.

EBay Inc. reported a 69 percent surge in profits, but analysts said the online auction house's period of rapid growth may be fading. EBay's shares were off $2.77, at $54.73, on the Nasdaq Stock Market.

"I think a lot of the expectations are already priced in the numbers," said Neil Massa, equity trader at John Hancock Funds. "Companies not only have to do better, they have to guide higher.... But earnings overall have been fine, and the economic numbers point to a recovery."

Sun was down 9 cents at $3.54 in heavy trading on the Nasdaq after reporting a wider-than-expected loss. The computer maker continues to struggle with weak demand and questions about its strategy.

DoubleClick plunged $2.80 to $9.44 after the online advertising company gave an outlook for its fourth quarter performance that missed Wall Street's estimates.

Ahold, the Dutch-based global food retailer, saw its U.S.-listed shares drop 54 cents to $9.52 after the company offered a grim outlook for its business, the first time it has discussed performance since a recent accounting scandal.

Micron Technology Inc. fell 14 cents to $12.69 after a downgrade by a UBS analyst. The disappointing corporate news outweighed several encouraging economic indicators. The Commerce Department reported that residential construction rose in September from the previous month, climbing to the second-highest level so far this year (leading economic indicator).

The report reinforced hopes that a strong housing market, which is being fueled in part by historically low interest rates, is helping to drive the economy out of its doldrums.

*(Seth Sutel, "StocksDrop on Earnings Disappointments," AP Business, October 18, 2003)*

## A FEW GOOD STOCKS

It was 1902 when S. A. Nelson made the statement cited in the introduction to Part 5: "It is easier to follow a few stocks well than it is to follow a well full of stocks." Nelson was an investor and, as noted, a friend of Charles Dow, founder of Dow Jones & Company. He was a publisher and an author of *The A.B.C. of Stock Speculation*. For many years Nelson had watched investors knocking themselves out trying to analyze and track too many different stocks. When an investor analyzes too many stocks, it can lead to information overload.

Keeping up with daily changing events quickly becomes impossible, and many are whipsawed on both sides of a price move. They buy at the top of a frenzied move and become disillusioned as the price turns and falls. Finally, they sell out at the bottom, only to see the price rise again.

The solution to information overload is to learn a great deal about a small number of stocks, the potential winners. Whether you follow three, five, or 10 companies doesn't really matter; what matters is that you learn a lot about these companies. Understanding the information that will improve the price performance of these companies will enable an investor to select better winners.

# CHAPTER 36

# Never Get Married to a Stock

Investors tend to get married to just a few types of stock. It might be the stock of a company they once worked at or the stock of a company that has a new miracle product: "This company has a product that will automatically cool a can of soda pop." It is often the stock they end up being frustrated with and stay with until death, usually the death of the company. But they are willing to stay with it, through thick and thin, sickness and health, etc.

The ideas behind new businesses are often exciting—one might even say irresistible. Sometimes the management has a celebrity working for them in some capacity. Frequently it is an individual with a background in something other than business. A heart surgeon can be the best in the country but make a terrible corporate president.

A lot of money goes into these start-up companies. When the stock is issued, its price might run up for a short while. But before long the stock has dropped back to the original price and below. Often, the stock languishes for several years with very little movement. It doesn't perform well for many reasons, some of which are explained below.

## WHY COMPANIES SOMETIMES UNDERPERFORM

### No Earnings

New start-up companies are frequently struggling on a small amount of money left over from paying off the venture capital group that brought the stock public. The companies may have been publicly traded for a year or more, but it could be three to five years before they show any real earnings. No earnings means cashflow problems, debt problems, supply problems, and a host of other difficulties requiring cash. Not enough money is often the main reason new companies fail.

## Poor Management

New companies can fail for lack of management, either in amount or experience. The world's greatest physician might not make a good CEO. A former astronaut or famous athlete does not necessarily have the ability to guide a company through its difficult early years. Ideally, upper management should come from a similar business or at least have a solid background in business. Often, high-profile professionals are too accustomed to having details handled for them without the need for them to fight for results. In contrast, with a new company it's usually a battle for results from the top of the organization to the bottom.

Investors sometimes get married to the stocks of larger, well-established companies as well. Usually this is a case in which they have been employed by the company at one time or another. They buy the stock with its price dropping and hang on to it because they know how "well run" the company has been in the past. In fact, it might have been well run when the investor worked for the company, but times have changed. Why else would it be having difficulties? The company is no longer well run, or has been unable to adapt to changes in the marketplace.

## Limited Product Line

New companies may be ahead of their time and may not yet have a realistic market. Sometimes a product gets stuck in the development phase—forever. In some cases there might not even be any intent to actually bring the current finished product to market. It is possible that the stock has been issued for public sale for the purpose of returning capital to the venture capitalist. A company without a working product might hope to pick one up along the way. How different is that from Microsoft's earliest days?

## Insufficient Financing

New companies might have trouble getting proper financing to successfully manufacture the product and supply it in sufficient quantities to fill orders. It comes back to not enough money again, still the number one problem.

## Lawsuits

Start-up companies are frequently engaged in lawsuits from unhappy employees, vendors, or moneylenders. Another source of lawsuits is patent infringement. Sometimes these lawsuits get nasty and time-consuming, which can tie up assets and time. In addition, they can hamper the ability of management to keep the start-up company going; the larger company, in comparison, has the resources to make it through these difficulties.

Companies with problems like these are often the stocks some investors buy and never want to sell. The price drops, and still investors hold on, thinking they might get lucky. Sometimes luck will prevail and the company will recover, but this can take several years. The gain on the investment might not be worth the wait. It is usually better for the investor to take the loss and move on to other opportunities.

## The Example of Western Union

The unfortunate decline of Western Union in the 1980s was a great disappointment to many former employees who bought the stock when it began to head down and then lost a lot of money as the price continued to drop.

Rather than, out of blind loyalty, buying the stock of a company an investor once worked for, he or she should evaluate the company and its competitors.

Actually, an individual might know even more about the competition than about the future of a company they used to work for, even recently. In fact, it often could be better to invest in the stock of a competitor.

Although a case can be made for holding a stock when the price has declined severely, getting married to a stock, then staying with it through thick and thin, can be a dangerous strategy. Buy and sell decisions in the stock market need to be made with logic and reason, without emotion.

# CHAPTER 37

# Act Quickly, Study at Leisure

**A** question from a customer to a broker might go like this:

"That's right. I want to sell 500 shares of IBM at the market. By the way, how's Apple doing? And Intel—what is Intel doing now?"

When a market order is being placed is not the time to check on other information. Once the broker has read back the order, it should be placed immediately. It is just not the time to check other quotes. Market price is good only until the next transaction. It could change and go against the trade. In the time it takes to place an order, hundreds or thousands of other orders could be coming in ahead of it and hammer the price down or push it unexpectedly higher.

The shares of many stocks can have abrupt moves during the day. Sometimes $5 or $10 moves can happen in moments. Certainly that's motivation enough for the investor to avoid any unnecessary delays. Get the order placed and check on the action later.

The same concept can be extended to the decision to take action. Once a course has been decided upon, it should be acted on at the earliest opportunity. Waiting a day or even a few hours can change the situation to something entirely different. Study and planning strategy do not mix well with implementation. They should be done as separate activities. Doing so will help prevent taking actions based on partial information and will make an analysis more effective when planning strategy.

# CHAPTER 38

# Records Can Make Money

Record keeping can be an important investment. Records of trades, confirmation slips, and monthly statements can provide information that will actually be worth extra dollars. Reliable record-keeping systems can be important time savers. At tax time, nothing can be more frustrating than trying to find mislaid records of transactions to verify dividends and capital gains or losses.

## CERTIFICATES HELD

One of the biggest mistakes investors make is placing the stock certificate in a safe deposit box with no other records of the transaction. Years later the investors will wonder what the cost of the stock was at the time of purchase. To avoid this problem, the "confirmation" notice of the buy should be clipped to the stock certificate when it is stored. Doing so will prevent endless headaches when the stock is sold and it's time to calculate the capital gains.

The IRS has an easy method of figuring the cost basis when the owner is unable to do so for a stock. They consider the entire proceeds from the sale as capital gains and tax them accordingly. Needless to say, this action could be costly.

## IMPORTANT DOCUMENTS

Stock certificates that are sent out to the buyer are very important documents. They are similar to titles or property deeds. Although they can be replaced if lost, destroyed, or stolen, it takes time to do so. Significant losses can occur while the owner is waiting for the new certificates. Time is lost while a stop is placed on the old certificates and records are searched to ascertain whether the certificates have been previously sold.

If dividends are being reinvested, see if the company will hold the certificates in a special account and have them issued in lots of 100 shares or more. This will prevent your ending up with several hundred certificates, each worth two or three shares.

### Eventual Book Entry

Eventually, stock certificates will be eliminated, and all investment securities will be held in book-entry format. Many stock exchanges around the world have already taken this action. It could make confirmations and statements even more important than they are now.

## OPEN ORDERS

Save open order (good-till-canceled) notices, and match them to the open order cancellation notices when they arrive. When a limit order to buy or sell stock is placed, an open order notice is generated. (Over-the-counter securities do not necessarily generate this notice.) The note informs the customer as to the details on the GTC order. Check these notices carefully for accuracy, and keep the notice where it is accessible. It will help prevent your placing the order twice.

It can be irritating to sell the same stock twice and have to pay for the repurchase. When a buy or sell is executed, the open order notice should be placed with the confirmation of the trade. The notice should be clipped to the certificate if it is shipped out to the investor or filed in chronological order if the certificates are held at the brokerage firm in street name. The notices can be more important than old canceled checks, and they should be kept in a safe place for a reasonable length of time. Many investors keep them the same length of time as tax records.

## MONTHLY STATEMENTS

Monthly brokerage account statements are also important records and should be kept for a reasonable length of time. Twelve statements a year is not a lot of paper, but this is one of the reasons that it's not a good idea to have 125 mutual funds. Statements can be helpful in tracking down possible errors or figuring out the details of transactions.

# RECORDS ORGANIZATION

An organized system for keeping track of transaction records and certificates can save the investor time and money. The cost can be astronomical to have an accountant or lawyer sort out the details of transactions. Investors should think of record keeping as an important part of the investment process.

# CHAPTER 39

# Invest in What You Know Best

"Know thyself…"

WILLIAM SHAKESPEARE

**D**iversification in an investment portfolio is always advisable; however, investing in an industry or a company where the investor has been employed can be profitable also. If an investor works in the auto industry, for instance, it is logical for that investor to do some investing in automobile stocks. A person who has worked for Ford Motor Company for several years will undoubtedly have special insight into how the company works. With that background, an investor could also have a unique understanding of the vendors used by Ford. Working directly with a supplier provides knowledge of a company's ability to supply products and services that could be worth more than spending numerous hours analyzing that vendor's balance sheet.

A pharmacist should have insight into the potential growth of pharmaceutical companies, and an electrical engineer could do well investing in high-tech companies. Investing in companies related to the investor's background is logical, but it is not done often. Doctors invest in Aerospace stocks, aerospace engineers invest in drug companies, and drug company employees invest in high-tech computer companies.

## SIGNIFICANCE VS. PUBLIC RELATIONS

We're all more or less vulnerable to public relations, and since most investors are unfamiliar with what's real and what is window dressing, it is difficult to discern which information is significant. However, the same people often have tremendous firsthand knowledge about the workings of their own industry. They might have 10 or 20 years experience—experience that can be used as a basis for analysis. Their work experience gives them advantages not available to the stock analyst. Most good analysts would love the opportunity to work for 30 days in the companies they follow and do the work incognito. The knowledge gained would be priceless. However, analysts do not have the time for such an activity, much less the opportunity.

When an investor already has the work experience, it only makes sense to make good use of the knowledge. If the stocks selected do well, consider the profits a work-related bonus for using job-related information.

## KEEP AN EYE ON THE COMPETITION

Competitive companies might even be better targets. People sometimes know more about the competition than about their own companies. A person working for IBM might actually know more about Compaq, just as the Compaq employee might well know that IBM's most recent development will generate strong sales.

Investing in the stock of a competitor can be an excellent strategy. It offers these advantages:

- No emotional involvement
- Early observation of developments
- Easily followed financial growth
- Insight into problems

Investing in the stock of companies with which one has practical working knowledge will not guarantee success, but it can make the analysis more meaningful and improve the chances of success. In addition, an investor can keep an eye on the competition's successes and failures, which would also be a valuable resource for the investor's regular employment.

## LOOK FIRST TO WHAT YOU KNOW

The learning curve regarding investing is steep, and mistakes can be costly. Investing in companies an investor knows and understands significantly reduces the amount of information to learn. This can lead to quick understanding and fast decisions when it comes time to buy or sell the stock.

# PART VI

# Caution

The first chapter in this section, "Give Stop Orders Wiggle Room," simply means to place a stop order far enough away from the current trading price so as not to tempt the specialist or market maker into executing the order. Although sell stops are used, the preference is that they never be executed. You only want buy stops executed when the stock price is having a strong upward movement.

No matter what the indicators are currently saying, it's inevitable that something can happen to completely override and overrun them. A perfect example was the terrorist attack on the World Trade Center. A market that was beginning to indicate recovery from an economic recession suddenly turned south again.

The investor should always be wary of "penny stocks." There is a reason the price is that low. Unless you want to buy controlling interest and manage the company (not recommended), stay away from these kind of investments, no matter how tempting.

Simple advice, like be wary of stock tips (from anyone) or be careful with a margin account, is basic common sense. Many people are completely caught by surprise with their first margin call, and that should not be the case. Margin calls only happen when the margined stock price is dropping, information that is constantly available.

# CHAPTER 40

# Give Stop Orders Wiggle Room

**A** *stop order* is an order to buy or sell stock when it reaches or passes through a predetermined price. *Buy stop orders* are placed above the current trading price, and *sell stop orders* are placed below the current price. Once activated, the stop order becomes a *market order* that says the investor will make the trade at the best available price.

If you believe the price of a stock is going to drop an unacceptable amount, sell the stock. Don't even consider a stop order. Why give the money away when you don't have to? That is the most important rule of all sell stop orders. They should be used carefully and cautiously during times of uncertainty.

## WHEN USING STOPS

"Wiggle room" is important when placing stop orders—whether buying or selling stock. Essentially, it allows the stock price to move in "normal" market swings without activating the stop. Allowing for wiggle room means placing the stop order close enough to the current price to prevent a loss on a sell or activate a buy on an upward move, but far enough from the current price so it will be triggered only by a larger than normal move.

Orders are activated as market orders (unless limits are set) when the price is traded on or through the stop price.

When buying, the investor wants the buy stop to be activated only if the stock price is making a strong move upward. On the other side, no one really wants the sell stop order to be filled unless the price is declining at a disturbing rate. Consequently, the buy stop is usually placed closer to the current trading range than is the sell stop. It is good to give the sell stop enough room for the price to fall during a small correction without activating the stop.

## SELL STOP

### Not Two Bucks or 10 Percent

Some say place a sell stop two dollars away from the current price; others say take losses at 10 percent. The problem with these solutions is the probability that the orders will be executed. The two-dollar sell stop is so close to the current price that the exchange specialist can easily be tempted to tick the price down and execute the order. The specialist is allowed to do just that. And to lock all stops into a 10 percent loss is also not a good idea. Some stock prices will swing 10 percent every week, others every day. What does make sense is to look at a price chart such as the one shown in Figure 40-1, to see the price trading range.

The first strong support is at the $68 dollar level. Assuming we bought the stock at $75 a share, a $68 stop would not be out of order.

**F I G U R E   40–1**

Fed Ex Corporation, January 2000–March 2004

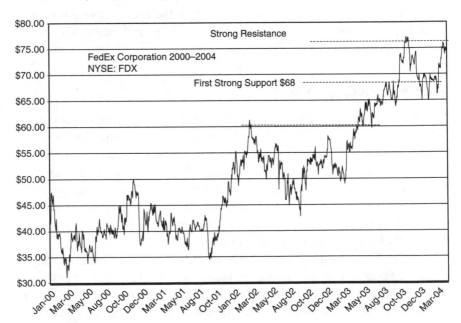

However, keeping in mind that a sell stop order is one that we do not want to see executed, wisdom would suggest a lower support level. The ideal would be a price that, once penetrated, drops considerably lower. The $60 to $65 range could be the ideal spot for a stop loss order. If the price drops through $65 a share, it is likely to drop much further.

### For Emergency Drops

Stop loss orders should be used for unexpected emergency price declines only. They should not be used as a way to sell stock. If the price is moving down gradually, either sell the stock at the market price or remove the sell stop order.

## BUY STOP

A buy stop is an aggressive buying approach that says you only want to buy the stock when the price is making a significant advance. Unlike the sell stop, this is an order you want to see executed, but only if the price is moving.

Placing the buy stop order also requires some study of the current trading range. The distance to establish between the buy stop price and the current trading price of the stock is a matter of personal decision, but it should be at least partially based on trading range analysis. A price chart can be of great assistance in selecting a good buy stop price. Just remember that the ideal situation is to catch the stock as the price moves and continues upward.

Look again at the price chart of FedEx in Figure 40-1. Current strong resistance is $75 to $76 a share. In the past, as resistance is penetrated the stock has shown advances. The stock price advanced from $45 to $60 in early 2002 and $60 to $75 in late 2003. If we place a buy stop at or just above the current top resistance level, the strategy should work well.

## LIKE MEDICINE, USE ONLY WHEN NECESSARY

An important point to remember about the use of buy or sell stop orders: If you believe a price will go up or will weaken and fall, forget using a stop and place a market order to buy or sell. It doesn't make sense to give the money away. Stops should be used only if there is considerable uncertainty.

## GOOD TILL CANCELED

Stop orders should be entered "good till canceled" (see Chapter 33 for a full explanation of GTC). Find out how long a GTC order will remain open, since the term has different meanings to various brokerage firms. Some orders stay in until the end of the month; others are canceled in a month. Stop orders can also be changed. They can be raised on the sell side if the price keeps rising or lowered on the buy side. A recent price chart should be consulted before an order is changed.

The sell stop can provide protection for profits, and it can also limit loss in a severe decline. But remember that it should be far enough away from the current price to avoid having it triggered by a minor move. It needs more wiggle room.

The buy stop can be placed closer to the current price because it is an order the investor wants triggered. Limit prices can also be placed on stops, but the limits might prevent the order from being filled. However, with a buy stop, a limit order can prevent the order from being filled on a sudden price move due to a takeover announcement.

## STOP LIMIT ORDER

A stop limit order, or OTC (over-the-counter) stop, is activated differently. Orders to buy are activated if there is a posted offer at or above the trigger price. Orders to sell are activated if there is a posted bid at or below the trigger price. Only some brokerage firms accept stop orders on OTC (Nasdaq) stocks. Check with your broker before trying to place an order.

# CHAPTER 41

# Indicators Can Meet Overriding Factors

"No matter what the current indicators are saying, they can be overridden by other, unexpected factors."

S. A. NELSON

In the second week of March 2004, an unconfirmed terrorist letter claimed the United States would be the object of another significant attack, similar to the 9/11 attack at the World Trade Center in New York. At the time, the stock market was building strength in an upward direction. Fundamentals were gaining strength in terms of reasonably positive earnings reports, and the market was showing growth in technical strength. The next few days looked different.

These were relatively high volume sell-offs, yet fundamentally, and technically there was no good reason for the secondary downtrend to appear. It was caused by the emotional overrun of the alleged "terrorist letter." This brings up two very frightening possibilities for the future: that these letters could be manufactured as a way to scare and manipulate the stock market; and if many such letters occur, it could become like the little boy who cried "wolf."

The Standard & Poor's 500 chart in Figure 41-1 provides a five-month context for the previously mentioned situation, in which positive indicators were overridden.

Clearly, the fear of another possible assault caused many investors to do some load lightening. Whether they were testing the solidarity of others or making changes based on their own fears is impossible to know. The

## TABLE  41-1

Overriding factors

|                       | Dow Industrials | S&P 500  | Nasdaq Composite |
|-----------------------|-----------------|----------|------------------|
| Monday, March 8       | −66.07          | −9.66    | −38.85           |
| Tuesday, March 9      | −72.52          | −6.62    | −13.62           |
| Wednesday, March 10   | −160.07         | −16.69   | −31.01           |
| Thursday, March 11    | −168.51         | −17.11   | −20.26           |

## FIGURE  41–1

Standard & Poor's 500 Index, January–May 2004

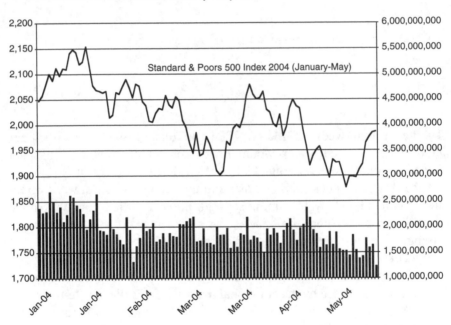

effect is the same. They were reflecting their concern about the economic
security of the stock market. The bullish uptrend turned and crossed the
trend line, creating a significant secondary downtrend that could become
a new primary direction.

Here are some other examples of events that can override positive
indicators:

- Funding for a large project (such as a corporate takeover) can fail to materialize at the last minute, sending the entire market into a spin.
- A U.S. Treasury bond auction might not go as well as expected, thereby causing interest rates to rise.
- An earthquake, flood, fire, hurricane, or other natural calamity can unexpectedly send the market down.
- War or a related event can break out and have negative global economic implications.
- A national scandal can appear in the news.
- The U.S. dollar can weaken and fall too low, or strengthen and become too high.
- Interest rates might be raised with the intention of slowing the economy.
- Economic distress in places other than the United States (such as the Asian crises in 1998) can have a negative impact on the stock market.
- An economic indicator such as the Producer Price Index (PPI), housing starts, or even inflation might be worse than expected.

Any of these events, as well as others, can appear suddenly and cause the stock market to change direction. It can happen even when all indicators are showing a strong and stable market.

## CURRENT EVENTS AND THE MARKET

It has been said that "information makes the market." More accurately, it is the reaction to the information that makes the market. The reaction is part of anticipation. The stock market will often rise on good news and fall on bad news. When the bad news is expected, the market often ignores the information because it had already been discounted. The market made its adjustment before the news appeared.

Understanding the economic implications of the news can help the investor know what to expect in the stock market. It's important to know what scares investors and what gets them excited with anticipation. The knowledge can help the investor comprehend the sudden market corrections or rallies.

Indicators, whether technical or fundamental, are important, but they can be—and often are—overridden by other events or situations.

# CHAPTER 42

# Beware the Penny Stock

*Penny stocks* have certain characteristics:

1. The price per share is low (usually five dollars or less, but can be higher).
2. The price will often go lower than one can imagine.
3. The low price makes these stocks targets for manipulation.
4. They tend to trade "thinly," sometimes going for weeks without a buy or sell.
5. At times it's nearly impossible to find buyers for those wanting to sell.
6. Reverse splits of 10-for-1 happen occasionally, to boost the price.
7. The risk is exceptionally high.

Although there is no set definition of penny stocks, many investors and brokers consider any stock selling for less than $10 a share to fit the category (five dollars and less is most common). Some prices on these stocks have dropped so low that they indeed sell for pennies. If shares are originally issued as penny stock, in many cases the company itself did the underwriting. Several million shares were probably issued and are not *blue sky* (approved for trading) in every state. Such conditions can make trading the stock difficult or impossible. It's not unusual for them to be fairly easy to buy and very difficult to sell, at any price.

## LURE OF MYTHS

Some investors believe (erroneously) that big, successful companies started out as penny stock. Myths about once being able to buy IBM at 50 cents a share and 3M at 19 cents a share crop up in occasional conversation. They talk about Mr. Hewlett and Mr. Packard building computers in their garage and using shares in the company as wages. Such beliefs are seldom based entirely on fact; rather, most are partial truths at best. The truth is, very few companies started out tiny and made it big, at least as far as penny stock is concerned.

The amount of risk in the low-price situation increases dramatically as the price of the stock drops even lower. It can be true that reward potential increases as risk increases, but this is often not the case with penny stocks. If a company whose stock is selling for about 50 cents has two or three employees left (who are looking for work), and they are unable to manufacture product or even ship product, that company will most likely go out of business and the stock price will drop to zero.

## I CAN AFFORD TO LOSE A THOUSAND

Despite the risk, some investors are attracted to stocks like these. The usual statement you hear is: "I thought I'd invest a thousand dollars on a flier. If I lose it, okay, but I might get lucky." In the vast majority of cases they don't get lucky, and the $1,000 is gone. Typically, the odds are better in horse racing or in a trip to Las Vegas, where they can at least get some entertainment for their money.

## PENNY STOCK RULES FROM THE SEC

The term "penny stock" generally refers to low-priced (below $5), speculative securities of very small companies. All penny stocks trade in the *OTC Bulletin Board* or the *Pink Sheets*—but not on national exchanges, such as the New York Stock Exchange, or the Nasdaq Stock Market.

Before a broker-dealer can sell a penny stock, SEC rules require the firm to first approve the customer for the transaction and receive from the customer a written agreement to the transaction. The firm must *furnish the customer a document* describing the risks of investing in penny stocks. The broker-dealer must tell the customer the current market quotation, if any, for the penny stock, and the compensation the firm and its broker will receive for the trade. Finally, the firm must send monthly account statements showing the market value of each penny stock held in the customer's account.

For more information, read our Compliance Guide to the Registration and Regulation of Brokers and Dealers. You may also want to review the penny stock rules (Securities Exchange Act Rules 15g-1 through 15g-9).

Before you consider investing in the stock of any small company, be sure to read our brochure, *Microcap Stock: A Guide for Investors*, available at http://www.sec.gov/answers/penny.htm.

# THINGS TO WATCH OUT FOR

## High-Pressure Sales Techniques

Investment in a legitimate emerging company is long term. A good little company is usually not going to skyrocket in a couple of weeks. Building a sound company takes years; you have a few days or weeks to decide whether the investment is right for you.

## Blind Pools and Blank Checks

Do not invest in any security without being told exactly how your money will be spent. Be sure you know which properties the company plans to buy with the offering proceeds and how much money is to be spent on management and promoters.

## Mismarked Trade Confirmations or New Account Cards

Be very wary if your trade confirmation is marked "unsolicited" if your broker did, in fact, solicit the trade. While it may be a simple mistake, unscrupulous penny stockbrokers often mark the confirmation as unsolicited to avoid the registration laws and the "fair, just, and equitable" standard. Watch for misstatements about your net worth, income, and account objectives as well. Investing in penny stocks is speculative business and involves a high degree of risk. Often, brokers will enhance the new account card to make it seem that you are suitable for a penny stock investment when you are not.

## Unauthorized Transactions

Be alert to placement in your account of securities you did not agree to purchase. In some instances a broker may try to pressure you into purchasing the stock, claiming that since you have the stock, you must pay for it. In some cases the broker is temporarily "parking" the securities in your account, perhaps to meet the minimum distribution of an IPO, or for any number of reasons. In some cases an unauthorized trade is simply a mistake, but in any case, complain immediately, both verbally and in writing to your broker, your broker's manager, and to the Securities Division.

### Buy Direct—Sell to Whom?

Sometimes penny stock can be purchased directly from the company, but the company might not be willing to buy the shares back when the investor is ready to sell. Unless the investor wants to own a controlling interest and manage the company, the super-low-priced penny stocks are usually best avoided.

## TAKING A FLYER

If you feel an overwhelming urge to "take a flyer" on a penny stock, one way to lower the risk is to buy only those shares on which you can obtain reliable research information about the company. Use the same fundamental analysis approach as you would use to buy blue-chip stocks for a long-term investment. This will at least give you some idea as to the company's prospects for recovery.

# CHAPTER 43

# Be Wary of Stock Ideas from a Neighbor

S. A. Nelson, author of the first book on the Dow theory (first published in the early 1900s), mentions the attraction of speculators to the stock market. Charles Dow, in 1900, also commented on the tendency of individuals to invest in a widely speculative stock, taking more risk than they would with their own businesses. Often the speculative investments are based on hearing about it from a friend.

Even today stockbrokers hear investors admit interest in a speculative issue of stock because "a neighbor told them." These stock recommendations can come with the best intentions, but should be viewed with much reservation.

## STOCK TIPS

The idea might be a good tip. One of the biggest problems is that it might have been a good tip some time (days or weeks) ago. The best stock ideas usually don't wait around for the investors to make their move. By the time the friend or neighbor has spread the word, it's too late to take any action. Learning more about the tip is a better strategy. Even though timing is often of the essence, answering a few questions can help prevent a costly mistake. Where did the idea originate? Could it be a rumor? Did a broker recommend the stock? Did the idea appear in a financial journal?

Sometimes a tip can be traced quickly to a reliable source; other times the source is illusive. The frustrating fact is that the greater the reliability of the source, the less time there is to take action. If the tip was discussed in the *Wall Street Journal*, *Investor's Business Daily*, the *New York Times*, or other such notable publications, the action has probably already occurred.

There are times when the action just gets going as a rumor is dis cussed, but this is the exception. If the source of the idea is a fellow worker or indeed a neighbor, some friendly conversation might shed valuable light on the insight. Was the source a vision, a dream, wishful thinking, or something else? Spending time to ask can save money.

It is also important to find out the nature of the tip. How speculative is it? Is it short term—a buyout rumor, by whom? Is it more long term— a merger, new contracts, or new revenue growth? Is the stock price less than $10 a share? Is the stock marginable, so you can borrow money to buy more? Also, if the stock cannot be bought on margin, then the number of other investors, especially institutions who will be interested, is limited.

Buyout rumors have a way of suddenly appearing and disappearing. Sometimes they are based on sound information; other times they are pure fabrication. The truth sounds as good as the falsehood. The stock price can rise just the same. There are also rumors that turn into announcements, only to run into a stone wall.

## RUMORS CAN BE COMPLETELY FALSE

NEW YORK—Rumors and errors happen on Wall Street all the time. But rarely do they involve the same stock at the same time—let alone with the bizarre, though temporary, effect they had on Oracle Corp.

At one point Thursday, amid rumors that the company's chief financial officer had quit, Oracle (NASDQ: ORCL) stock appeared to have dropped to $22.25 on the Nasdaq Stock Market, a plunge of 29 percent from Wednesday at 4:00 p.m., representing a loss of $50 billion in shareholder value. But the rumor was false. And the trade at $22.25 was an error. By day's end the official low of Oracle stock for the day was $27.25, a drop of 13 percent, and Jeffrey Henley, the chief financial officer of the Redwood Shores, Calif., software company, was still in place. At 4:00 p.m., Oracle was down $1.81, or 5.7 percent, at $28.56.

*(Greg Ip, "Trade Error, Rumors Hit Oracle Stock," Wall Street Journal Online, November 2, 2000, 4:00 P.M. PT, URL, http://zdnet.com.com/2100-11-525280.html)*

Accidents and mistakes will happen, but this rumor, which accompanied the error, was entirely false. An investor reacting too quickly could have made an unfortunate trade that would later be regretted.

# RUMORS CAN BE TOTAL FABRICATIONS

Do you smell that? It's the smell of scores of investors burned by another online hoax involving phony company news.

The latest case: a news release on the Internet *this morning* claimed Emulex (EMLX: Nasdaq— news) would restate earnings and report a loss rather than a profit. The stock, in turn, plunged 57% before it was halted on the Nasdaq Stock Market.

Emulex reopened after the hoax was detected and the stock regained most of its value, closing down 7⁵⁄₁₆, or 6.5%, at 105¾. But in the interim, many investors dumped the shares first and asked questions later. Among the many questions now being asked: How can investors protect themselves from making the same mistake twice?

Market-moving online hoaxes have happened before: In February, hackers broke into Aastrom Biosciences Web site and posted a phony notice about a merger with rival Geron. And in April 1999 a PairGain employee posted a bogus story online saying that the company had agreed to be acquired. In a market climate that sees an ever-increasing number of investors monitoring the latest news releases, it's likely to happen again.

*(Tim Arango and Dagen McDowell, "Once Bitten: Lessons from the Emulex Hoax," The Street.com, August 25, 2000, 5:22 P.M. ET)*

## DECISION MAKING

Here are some questions to ask in reaching a decision about a stock tip:

- How does the purchase/sell fit into the investment strategy?
- How much risk currently exists with other investments?
- What proportion of the portfolio is in the risk category?

When assessing a stock tip, consider how the stock fits into the broader investment strategy and goals. If some funds have been established as speculative money, by all means make use of them. However, limiting and controlling risk whenever possible is always prudent.

## RISK AND REWARD

Investing in the stock market always has an element of risk. Some risk is low and often is lessened over time. Other risk is high and is strictly short term. Greater risk does not always bring greater rewards. Before investing in high-risk, speculative situations, it is worthwhile to ask a few extra questions and do some research on the initial source of information. This will not eliminate risk, but it can allow you to at least enter an investment being aware of the risk, an awareness that may prompt you to go in another direction.

Whether it's a stock tip from a neighbor, a friend, or a hot tip from an Internet chat room, tips are always fraught with high risk and often little in the way of rewards. They should be approached with reserved skepticism.

# CHAPTER 44

# Heavily Margined, Heavily Watched

To *margin* is to borrow money using stocks or other securities that have been fully paid for as collateral. These borrowed funds can be used for any purpose (the cash can be withdrawn), although the money is most commonly used to buy more stock or other securities. A margin can be a useful tool to leverage investments for greater profits. In essence, an investor puts up one-half the value of the stock that he or she purchases on margin.

## KNOW THE MARGIN RULES

The Federal Reserve Board and many self-regulatory organizations (SROs), such as the NYSE and NASD, have rules that govern margin trading. Brokerage firms can establish their own requirements as long as they are at least as restrictive as the Federal Reserve Board and SRO rules. Here are some of the key rules you should know:

### Before You Trade: Minimum Margin

Before trading on margin, the NYSE and NASD, for example, require you to deposit with your brokerage firm a minimum of $2,000 or 100 percent of the purchase price, whichever is less. This is known as the "minimum margin." Some firms may require you to deposit more than $2,000.

### Amount You Can Borrow: Initial Margin

According to Regulation T of the Federal Reserve Board, you may borrow up to 50 percent of the purchase price of securities that can be purchased on margin. This is known as the "initial margin." Some firms require you to deposit more than 50 percent of the purchase price. Also be aware that not all securities can be purchased on margin.

### Amount After You Trade: Maintenance Margin

After you buy stock on margin, the NYSE and NASD require you to keep a minimum amount of equity in your margin account. The equity in your account is the value of your securities less how much you owe your brokerage firm. The rules require you to have at least 25 percent of the total market value of the securities in your margin account at all times. This is called the "maintenance requirement." In fact, many brokerage firms have higher maintenance requirements, typically between 30 and 40 percent, and sometimes higher, depending on the type of stock purchased.

Here's an example of how maintenance requirements work. Say you purchase $16,000 worth of securities by borrowing $8,000 from your firm and paying $8,000 in cash or securities. If the market value of the securities drops to $12,000, the equity in your account will fall to $4,000 ($12,000 − $8,000 = $4,000). If your firm has a 25 percent maintenance requirement, you must have $3,000 in equity in your account (25 percent of $12,000 = $3,000). In this case, you do have enough equity because the $4,000 in your account is greater than the $3,000 maintenance requirement.

But if your firm has a maintenance requirement of 40 percent, you would not have enough equity. The firm would require you to have $4,800 in equity (40 percent of $12,000 = $4,800), and your $4,000 is less than the firm's $4,800 maintenance requirement. As a result, the firm may issue you a "margin call," since the equity in your account has fallen $800 below the firm's maintenance requirement.

## UNDERSTAND MARGIN CALLS: YOU CAN LOSE MONEY FAST, WITH NO NOTICE

If your account falls below the firm's maintenance requirement, your firm generally will make a margin call to ask you to deposit more cash or securities into your account. If you are unable to meet the margin call, your firm will sell your securities to increase the equity in your account up to or above the firm's maintenance requirement.

Always remember that your broker may not be *required* to make a margin call or otherwise tell you that your account has fallen below the firm's maintenance requirement. Your broker may be able to sell your securities at any time *without consulting you first*. Under most margin agreements, even if your firm offers to give you time to increase the equity in your account, it can sell your securities without waiting for you to meet the margin call.

## ASK YOURSELF THESE QUESTIONS

- Do you know that margin accounts involve a great deal more risk than cash accounts where you fully pay for the securities you purchase? Are you aware you may lose more than the amount of money you initially invested when buying on margin? Can you afford to lose more money than the amount you have invested?
- Did you take the time to read the margin agreement? Did you ask your broker questions about how a margin account works and whether it's appropriate for you to trade on margin? Did your broker explain the terms and conditions of the margin agreement?
- Are you aware of the costs you will be charged on money you borrow from your firm and how these costs affect your overall return?
- Are you aware that your brokerage firm can sell your securities without notice to you when you don't have sufficient equity in your margin account?

For more information about margin trading, visit the Web site of NASD, where you can read from a collection of articles and other resources: http://www.sec.gov/investor/pubs/margin.htm.

## MARGIN RULES, REGULATIONS, AND REQUIREMENTS

The rules, regulations, and requirements regarding margin accounts come from three sources:

1. The Federal Reserve Board sets margin requirements as part of monetary policy. These are referred to as Fed requirements.
2. Stock exchanges also set margin requirements that their member firms are required to observe, and when the exchange setting the requirement is the New York Stock Exchange (NYSE), most or all firms observe the requirement whether or not they are NYSE member firms. These are known as exchange requirements.
3. Brokerage firms set their own, more rigorous margin requirements, and their margin allowances are more restrictive than the Federal Reserve's. They are allowed to do this in order to limit their risk. These rules and regulations are known as house requirements.

## INTEREST CHARGES

Brokerage firms make money on margin accounts from the interest they charge on the loans and also from commissions on the larger transaction sizes that buying on margin allows. However, lending money carries risks for the brokerage firms similar to the risks that banks face when lending; the borrower may not want to, or may not be able to, pay back the money borrowed.

## REGULATION T

Current Regulation T requires that investors pay for 50 percent of the value at the time of the transaction. A minimum of $2,000 equity is also required to be in the account. The $2,000 can be in the form of cash or fully paid marginable securities. For example, financing to buy 200 shares of POW Corporation at $106 per share could be as follows:

| | |
|---|---|
| Total cost: | $21,200 |
| Investor puts in: | −10,600 |
| Amount borrowed: | $10,600 (margin debit) |

## STOCK PRICE RISES

If the price of POW Corporation rises to $150 per share, its total market value will be $30,000. The investor owes only the margin debit and whatever interest has accumulated (the debit is a loan, and interest is charged only for the days the debt is outstanding). In the POW Corporation, for example, the investor still owes the debit of $10,600, plus interest:

| | |
|---|---|
| Current Market value: | $150 per share |
| Total market value: | $30,000 |
| Debit owed: | −10,600 |
| Investor's equity: | $19,400 |

    If the investor sells the position and takes profits, the picture would look like this:

| | |
|---|---|
| Investor's equity: | $19,400* |
| Original investment: | −10,600 |
| Profit: | $ 8,800 |

*The debit remains constant. It is unaffected by market price changes.

- After the margin debit is repaid.
- Note: There will also be interest charges and commissions for the trades.

Essentially, the investor has doubled the gain through leverage by buying twice as many shares, with half of the total amount purchased by means of a loan. Although the maximum of 50 percent loan value is used in this example, it is allowable to borrow less than that amount.

## STOCK PRICE DROPS

Using a margin is fine as long as the price of the stock rises. The problems with margins occur when the price begins to drop. What if, instead of rising in price, POW Corporation were to fall to $50 a share?

```
200 POW Corporation
$50 per share market value:    $10,000
Margin debit owed:            -10,600*
Investor's equity:             ($600)
```

*The debit remains constant. It is unaffected by market price changes.

If the investor sold out at $50 a share, not only would the original investment of $10,600 be lost, but the investor would also owe an additional $600. This is reason enough to watch margined positions carefully.

## MAINTENANCE CALL

In reality, the investor would usually receive a *margin maintenance call* before this low level was ever reached. However, in a rapidly declining market, there might not be enough time to deliver the additional funds or fully paid marginable securities necessary to cover the maintenance call. Maintenance requirements can be anywhere from 25 to 50 percent equity—a 30 percent equity requirement is common for many stocks—of the current market value or $2,000 (whichever is greater). Although the calculations can become complicated with variations in a margin portfolio, they are based on the following simple formula:

$$Equity = market\ value - debit$$

In other words, an investor can expect a margin maintenance call for the deposit of additional funds or fully paid, marginable securities if the market price of the stock falls below the borrowed amount (debit) plus 25 to 30 percent (the actual amount depends on brokerage firm requirements).

## UNMET CALLS MET

If the required margin is not maintained, the brokerage firm has every right to sell securities in the account to cover the amount or prevent further loss, without notifying the investor beforehand. This was a common occurrence during the 1987 crash. Investors, some of whom were on vacation, returned to find their stock portfolios, once worth hundreds of thousands of dollars, totally gone. In fact, many still owed substantial amounts of money to the brokerage firm.

"Heavily margined, heavily watched" is a market axiom well worth remembering and following. It is also prudent to protect margin positions. Total protection is not possible, but a few precautions can lessen the blow of a severe decline.

## PROTECTION

Protect the margin position with careful and deliberate attention. Brokers are often amazed at the number of investors who make stock purchases just before leaving on vacation. It's as if there was some special list of things to do: stop the mail, load the car, get the kids, and buy some stock. In fact, it is usually not the best time to buy any stock, and can be exactly the wrong time to increase a margin position. A lot can happen to the stock market in a week or two. Most people leaving for vacation have enough to do without keeping an eye on the market.

## MARGIN STRATEGIES

Margin can be used with minimal risk and maximum impact, but doing so requires care and attention. Margin positions can be well maintained by implementing a few simple strategies.

### Daily Observation
Keep an eye on the developing market situation by computer, communication with the broker, or checking the newspapers.

### Extra Precautions
Take extra precautions when leaving town on a vacation or business trip. Consider making special arrangements with the broker to have someone bring money or fully paid securities to cover any possible maintenance calls. Keep in touch. It can be a good idea to reduce or totally pay off a margin debt if your trip is planned for an extended period.

Place Protective Orders
This could be a good situation for stop-loss orders wherever possible.

Sell Margined Positions
Keep only the fully paid securities, and reduce the debit to zero. This
would eliminate the possibility of margin calls.

Be Extra Cautious with a Short Position
A short position has a potentially unlimited risk, since there is no limit to
how high the price of a stock can rise. Carefully placed buy-stop orders
can help control this risk.

## USE MARGIN FOR LEVERAGE

Margin can be a useful tool for leverage when buying securities. It should
be used carefully and deliberately. Like all investment strategies, an
investor must have a basic understanding of the workings of a margin
before using this leverage. It is possible to learn more about using a margin by asking the broker for information, finding books on the subject, or
searching the Internet.

# CHAPTER 45

# Beware the Triple Witching Hour

"'Tis now the very witching time of night when churchyards yawn and hell itself breathes out contagion to this world."

WILLIAM SHAKESPEARE, *HAMLET*

The third Friday of every month is the last day to trade stock options. Options actually expire on Saturday, but it is the expiration of trading that can cause concern. Unusual volatility can occur in this third week, due to the unwinding of options positions. At times this volatility seems unrelated to any of the usual market indicators, as though it exists for itself.

## A LITTLE LESS SCARY NOW

- March
- June
- September
- December

These are the months when options, futures, and index options all expire on the same third Friday of the month. In recent years, by spreading out the due dates over Thursday and Friday, the options exchanges have diluted the impact, and new regulations and stricter controls have helped to moderate the situation. Trading circuit breakers, for instance, now limit huge gains or losses in the stock markets, thereby making it more difficult for insti-

tutions and short sellers to drive the market down. But the potential for a
hyperactive market during these times is still with us.

Volume still increases, but the point moves are not nearly as severe as
back in the 1980s. Even in the down market of 2001, the Triple Witching
dates did not appear to be a big event. Any significant drop in the Dow
Average came days or weeks after the traditionally torturous Fridays.
Figure 45-1 notes the market's reaction on those dates from 2001 to 2004.

## BAD NEWS CAN HAVE AN IMPACT

If significant economic news comes out at the same time as the expirations
occur, the volatility can be magnified. But that can confuse the issue, and
it's difficult to tell if it was news that made the market volatile or if the
Triple Witching was more to blame.

The moves involve large traders changing positions from index
options and futures to other positions or the actual stocks. An individual
investor should be aware of the event, since the days still have some teeth.
Although the serious decline of the stock market appears to have been moderated, there is some market decline after most Triple Witching events.

## F I G U R E   45–1

Dow Industrial Average and Volume, April 2001–January 2004

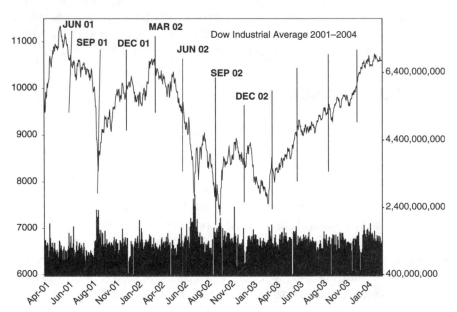

# PART VII

# Surprises

A good surprise in the stock market is not what we'll discuss in this section. That would be the positive earnings surprise where analysts were expecting 23 cents a share and the quarter came in at 42 cents a share.

A stock split, which we'll deal with, is a neutral surprise. Although many people consider them positive events, the facts are quite different. Some are positive for a short time and then neutral or even negative.

Most other surprises in the stock market are bad surprises. All of a sudden the hot stock is down ten bucks and heading lower. It might be because of fraud or because the company is facing a major lawsuit.

Safety in numbers can be found with well-run investment clubs. From such clubs the investor can learn a great deal about the stock market. Serving on analysis committees and making presentations to the rest of the group can be quite instructive and worth checking out.

# CHAPTER 46

# Avoid Heavy Positions in Thinly Traded Stocks

The terms "heavy traded" and "thinly traded" can mean different things to different investors. A heavy position for one might be 5,000 to 10,000 shares; for another it could mean a few hundred shares. Thinly traded might describe a stock that doesn't trade on some days, or it could describe a stock that trades less than 5,000 shares a day. The terms are not absolute; however, they should be considered together as "heavy position and thinly traded."

## YOU CAN BUY, BUT NOT SELL

A heavy position in a thinly traded stock might be easy to buy but difficult to sell. "Thinly traded" can refer to low volume, or to shares that do not necessarily trade every day. When they trade, they might trade several thousand shares or 200 shares. Many stock traders consider anything less than 10,000 shares a day as thin.

## USUALLY LOW-PRICED

Thinly traded stocks also tend to have relatively low prices, often below three dollars a share. A problem can arise in this way: Although it is relatively easy to buy 10,000 shares of a thinly traded stock, it could be difficult to sell the position. Selling might necessitate breaking the block into smaller segments of 5,000 or 3,000 shares, or even 1,000 shares. All of those shares "hitting the bid" (pushing the price lower by selling) can be damaging to profits. The investor can also be charged additional commissions if the buys or sells cannot be executed on the same day.

The following comes to us from *BusinessWeek*:

> It has become almost routine. On Nov. 13, the U.S. Attorney in Brooklyn charged 13 people—brokers, mob associates, and officials of two brokerage firms—with manipulating the prices of thinly traded microcap stocks. On the same day, in New Jersey, federal authorities announced a similar indictment. And then, on Nov. 25, came this bombshell: A federal grand jury in Manhattan handed up an indictment charging 19 people with multiple counts of racketeering and securities fraud. Among the accused were stock promoters, alleged mobsters, corporate officials, and six brokers at a firm that had managed to avoid the limelight, Meyers Pollock Robbins Inc. Not since the insider-trading scandals of the 1980s has Wall Street faced such a sustained legal juggernaut.
>
> "Chop" is slang for spread—the difference between the prices the brokerages pay for stocks and the prices at which they are sold to the public. In the world of the "chop houses" that sell these stocks, the real spreads often bear no relation to the numbers that appear on stock-quote machines. Often the stock is obtained by the brokers from corporate insiders or offshore accounts at a fraction of the price listed on the quote terminals. They then sell it to the public, illegally, at massive, undisclosed markups. It's fraud of the most fundamental kind. The public doesn't know that they are buying stocks that are worth nothing more than the pennies shelled out by their brokers.

> *(Gary Weiss, "Investors Beware: Chop Stocks Are on the Rise," an inside look at how scamsters are taking billions from small investors, updated December 4, 1997 by bwwebmaster, McGraw-Hill Companies, Inc.).*

## BE CAREFUL ON THE PHONE

Brokers gather business by making "cold calls," which means they call from a phone book, a reverse directory, or another listing and sell investments to people they have never met. This activity is not illegal in the United States, although it is illegal in some other countries. Most cold callers are reputable brokers just trying to make a living, and they are trying to meet the investor's objectives. However, the chop-stock brokers couldn't care less about objectives other than their own. They are trained for the quick, hard sell. Their philosophy is to "let the buyer beware."

Chop-stock brokers are difficult to control. The new promoters gain control over cheap stock, or dominate the markets for thinly traded stocks, and then push them on the public, using crews of brokers reporting to them.

Neither the NASD and Securities and Exchange Commission's highly visible campaign against small-stock abuses nor the recent spate of criminal prosecutions have made a significant impact on chop houses. Although regulators have shut down a handful of cold-calling powerhouses, the vast majority of questionable firms—totaling perhaps 200 nationwide, according to state securities regulators—remain untouched.

## USE CAUTION TAKING SPECULATIVE POSITIONS

Although thinly traded stocks might be worth a light speculative position of a few hundred shares held for a long-term investment, they should probably not make up a significant position for short-term trading. Also, investors should learn about the company (make a visit) and not buy stock on the basis of some cold-calling "cowboy" who will sell anything to anybody. Brokers are required to know their client's investment objectives. Thinly traded stocks will not fit well into a growth or income portfolio.

## RELATED TO PENNY STOCK

Penny stocks are often thinly traded and easily lend themselves to fraud and unreasonable markups that are almost impossible to detect. The stock markets depend on investors at all levels being essentially honest and straightforward. The problem is that a dishonest firm or broker can come along and raise havoc just by ignoring some of the rules. It takes a while for them to be caught, and in the meantime they can do millions of dollars in damage. Thinly traded and penny stocks are prudently best avoided.

# CHAPTER 47

# Fraud Is Unpredictable

**A**nything can happen in the stock market. It is possible to research and select a stock that is about to double or triple in price, and it is possible to buy a stock that is about to fold the tent and head toward the cellar. The most difficult bad news to anticipate is fraud. Investors buy stock based on the assumption that the company is being straightforward with their financial information. Because of this assumed honesty, it is nearly impossible to see fraud coming. The devastating impact of fraud hits the professional investor as well as the individual.

Take a look at what happened to WorldCom and Enron (Figure 47-1) after fraud accusations were made.

World Com was nearly a "six bagger" increasing to six times its mid-1994 price. In February of 1999 it looked like it could go up forever. Enron had soared ever upward from $13.50 to more than $87.00 a share, and they both dropped off the radar. Pity the poor investor who bought WorldCom in March 1999 and then later bought Enron in September 2000.

## SOMETIMES IT'S NOT FRAUD

Individual stock prices can drop suddenly with no immediate explanation. News announcements might be slow to come forward. The drop might have just been a fluke. A large investor decides to do some portfolio rearrangement, another large investor sees a significant sell and adds to the melee.

**F I G U R E  47–1**

WorldCom and Enron, 1994–2004

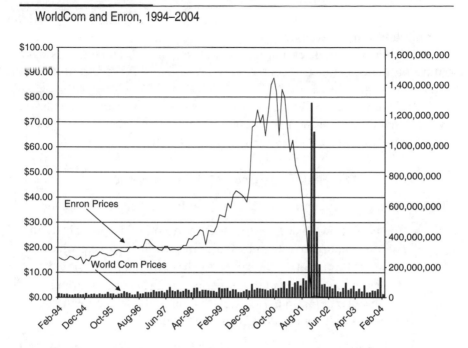

On occasion, investors will bring lawsuits against companies because the price has dropped. Although this is not a favorable event, it is not the same as fraud.

## SELL SOON

It can be prudent to quickly sell at the first sign of fraudulent activity. Most institutional investors will quickly sell all or part of their positions, which causes the price to plummet. This is why it is important to find out as soon as possible why a stock has had a sudden, severe drop in price. The investor must discover the content of the bad news and take action.

## USE CARE WITH INTERNET TRANSACTIONS

In recent years the Securities and Exchange Commission (SEC) has become concerned about fraudulent securities available via the Internet. Apparently, some unscrupulous individuals are surfing right into people's life savings. Here are some of the approaches they use:

## The Pyramid Scheme

The first people entering the pyramid often get big returns, but investors entering later usually lose everything. The "high returns" come from new investors and goes to the earlier investors. Eventually it all collapses. One online promoter claimed recently that you could "turn five dollars into $60,000 in just three weeks."[1]

According to the SEC, this was just an electronic version of the classic pyramid scheme. It's well suited to online computing, where a lawbreaker can send messages to 1,000 people with the touch of a mouse button.

## The Risk-Free or Low-Risk Scheme

Here are some other approaches used by the Internet scam artists:

- "Exciting, Low-Risk Investment Opportunities" to participate in exotic-sounding investments, including wireless cable projects, prime bank securities, and eel farms have been offered online.
- One promoter attempted to get people to invest in a fictitious coconut plantation in Costa Rica, claiming the investment was similar to a CD, with a better interest rate.

At times these cons will misrepresent the risk by comparing their opportunity to something an investor considers safe, such as bank certificates of deposit. The obvious intent is to make the investor comfortable. If it's "just like a CD," there's nothing to worry about. In the United States, to be "just like a CD," an investment would have to be backed by the FDIC. up to the first $100,000. Anything less than that isn't like a CD. Some schemes don't even have an investment product to sell. They just have people send in money.

## The Pump-and-Dump Scam

It is common to see Internet messages posted online urging readers to buy a stock quickly because it is poised for rapid growth. Often the writer claims to have "inside" information about an impending development or will claim to use an "infallible" combination of economic and stock market data to pick stocks.

According to the SEC, the promoter might be an insider who works for the company and will gain by selling shares after the stock price is pumped up by gullible buyers.

---

[1] Example *SEC Investor Beware,* Securities Exchange Commission, Office of Investor Education and Assistance, June 1996.

The Internet advice might also be a warning to sell a stock. It might be a short seller who stands to gain if the price goes down. The ploy is often used with little known, thinly traded stocks. The individual investor is left holding the bag after a whirlwind of activity.

## INVESTIGATE BEFORE INVESTING

Print out a copy of any online solicitation. Make certain to copy the Internet address (URL), and note the date and time that you saw the offer. Save the printout in case you need it later. Check with your state securities regulator or the SEC to see if they have received any complaints about the company, its managers, or the promoter. Don't assume that people are who they claim to be. The investments that sound the best could be figments of someone's crooked imagination and nothing else.

Check with a trusted financial adviser, your broker, or your attorney about any investment you learn about online. You can also ask the promoter where the firm is incorporated. Contact that state's secretary of state and ask if the company is indeed incorporated with them, with a current annual report on file.

Don't assume the access provider or online service has approved or even screened the investment. They don't do that sort of thing. Anyone can set up a Web site or advertise on the Internet without any check into legitimacy or untruthfulness.

Before you invest, always obtain written financial information such as a prospectus, annual report, offering circular, and financial statements. Compare the written information to what you've read online, and watch out if you're told that the information is not available.

If a company is not registered or has not filed a Form D with the SEC, call the SEC's Office of Investor Education and Assistance at (202) 942-7040 or contact your state securities regulator. You can also visit the SEC's Web site at www.sec.gov or contact them by e-mail. Regular mail can be sent to:

Securities Exchange Commission
Office of Investor Education & Assistance
450 Fifth Street, NW Mail Stop 11-2
Washington, DC 20549

## FRAUD IS DIFFICULT TO SPOT

The advice heard many times, "If it sounds to good to be true, it probably is," is easy to think of but often difficult to follow. In the past it might have kept many people away from companies like Microsoft, Apple Computer, or Winnebago when they first started. They were not fraudulent investments in any way, and that is what the scam artist is counting on to gain the investor's confidence.

A personal visit to a company can be helpful, but again it doesn't ensure the integrity of the information. Companies tend to be good at putting on a dog and pony show for investors and brokers. Even the worst of companies can usually put together a good show for an interested audience. Often, the best information about a company comes from outside sources that are in a position of being more objective.

Usually, the best defense is to avoid companies where there is any doubt involved. If evidence of fraud appears, sell out quickly and take the loss.

# CHAPTER 48

# There's (Almost) Always a Santa Claus Rally

Santa Claus is comin' to town … and to the stock market. To the purist, any rally between the Thanksgiving holiday and Christmas Day is a Santa Claus Rally. Actually, virtually any rally in the months of November or December is credited to the "jolly old elf." It's the buying season, a time when some retailers make their year profitable. Consumers go shopping with frenzy, and not only for a gift to place under a tree. Many excited shoppers also buy themselves presents. The Friday after Thanksgiving remains the busiest day of the year for retailers. Consumers have been saving their money and curbing their impulses just for this day. It's only natural that the buying frenzy would extend itself into the stock market.

## 10 YEARS OF RALLIES

There was not much of a rally in 1994, but the next five years more than made up for it, with a nearly continuous rally. What some called the rally of the century. The Dow Industrial Average climbed an incredible 11,489 points, with the Transportation Average gaining an outstanding 2,969 points. The S&P 500 Index was up 1,461 points, and the Nasdaq Index advanced 4,061 points (Figure 48-1).

In 1999 the rallies were strong in three of the four stock groups. The Transportation Average actually had a decline, possibly giving an early signal of weakness for what was to follow. The decline in 2002 followed an earlier rally that many would describe as Santa showing up early.

## FIGURE 48–1

10 years of rallies, 1994–2004

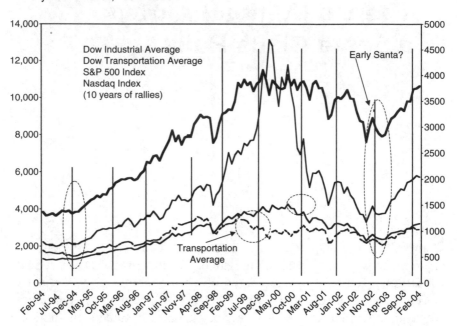

## ALWAYS A SANTA RALLY

There's no such thing as "always" for the fluctuations of the stock market. Because the market trades on anticipation of higher or lower prices, it frequently surprises investors with rallies or corrections. Although it is possible to have a bearish trend in the last two months of a year, there will likely be some kind of rally. Some of these rallies will be significant, others quite modest.

Table 48-1 details the changes in four market indexes during the final two months in the past 10 years. As you can see, in all but two instances there was in fact a Santa Rally.

There is a repetitive tendency of the stock market to rally between the months of November and December. An investor can take advantage of such rallies by patiently waiting for them to appear and then deciding to take a profit.

## TABLE 48-1

Santa Claus Rally Point Increases for 10 years

| Year | Dow Industrials | Dow Transports | S&P 500 | Nasdaq Index |
|------|-----------------|----------------|---------|--------------|
| 1994 | 95.2 | 11.64 | 5.58 | 1.64 |
| 1995 | 42.63 | 89.32 | 10.56 | 7.06 |
| 1996 | 73.43 | 35.15 | **−16.28** | 1.58 |
| 1997 | 85.12 | 56.54 | 15.03 | 30.20 |
| 1998 | 64.88 | 118.08 | 65.60 | 243.15 |
| 1999 | 619.31 | 67.48 | 80.34 | 733.15 |
| 2000 | 373.5 | 195.41 | 5.33 | **−127.4** |
| 2001* | 170.01 | 128.21 | 8.63 | 19.82 |
| 2002 | 499.06 | 100.55 | 50.54 | 149.03 |
| 2003 | 671.46 | 85.82 | 53.72 | 43.11 |

*Early rally

# CHAPTER 49

# A Stock Price Splits When It Gets Too High

It's kind of a combination of yes and no. On the no side is Warren Buffett with Berkshire Hathaway. The BRK.A shares at $93,500 a share and the BRK.B shares at $3,115 a share more than suggest that splitting is not a necessary function of a too-high price level. Even so, many companies will announce the reason for a two for one, three for one, or three for two, or some other forward split as necessary to lower the price to make the stock available to a larger group of investors.

## SPLIT TYPES

It's the *forward split* that is considered a neutral to positive event. On the other hand, a backward or *reverse split* is considered a very negative occasion. The reverse split lowers the number of shares and increases the current price. If you have 1,000 shares of stock at $1.00 per share, a 10-for-1 reverse split would leave 100 shares at $10.00 each. The problem is, the price usually doesn't stay at the new higher level for long, but drops back to the bottom.

## WHO HAS THE MOST SHARES

Microsoft's split in February of 2003 created 10 billion shares of stock. Still, Microsoft's split put the software company ahead of General Electric as having the most shares outstanding of any U.S. company. To give this some relative perspective, consider that the number 10 billion is:

- More than twice the Earth's age of 4.6 billion years
- The number of dollars airlines borrowed from the U.S. government after the September 11 attacks
- More dollars than most people have
- The estimated number of dollars Michael Jordan has contributed to the economy through the sale of shoes, tickets, and other items, according to *Fortune* magazine

Hyperbole aside, Microsoft's split is significant in that it happened at all. It is the first major technology firm to split its shares in 10 months, says Jon Johnson, chief market strategist of StockSplits.net. During the late years of the bull market, stock splits were nearly synonymous with tech stocks as prices soared. But when stocks are falling—and down to rock bottom prices, as is the case with many formerly leading tech firms—there is little reason for companies to split. The price is low enough just due to weakness. So the timing of the Microsoft split was a bit of a bullish signal, at least for the tech market, if not the market as a whole.

## BAD NEWS, GOOD NEWS

There are times when the announcement of a stock split seems to be for the purpose of softening the blow of bad news. Company ABC might make a great fanfare to announce a three-for-two split and then a couple of days later announce earnings weakness. Whether the strategy works is difficult to say, but it does happen.

## MESSY SPLITS

A forward split that is two for one, three for one, or sometimes five for one, is often just a clean split with nothing additional in the pot. But occasionally a stock will split five for four or four for three, with additional cash or preferred stock thrown in the kitty. These messy splits can be big headaches for professional investors, and they often avoid them altogether.

## BULLISH WITH ATTITUDE

A stock split announcement tends to convey a bullish attitude and a feeling that the company is doing something for the benefit of the investors. This benefit doesn't bear close examination, but it conveys a kind of corporate, warm, fuzzy feeling.

# CHAPTER 50

# Join the Club

**W**e could start a club. Get a bunch of people together, pool our money, and get rich together. Plus, we'd learn something about the stock market.

That's often the way it starts; someone suggests a club, talks up the idea to friends, neighbors, and other acquaintances. They meet monthly to discuss the market and stocks, as well as to make some investment decisions. Some clubs do well, some become famous or infamous (e.g., Beardstown Ladies), and other clubs fall apart the first year. The Internet is becoming a large resource for investment clubs, supplying research and other information to subscribers. Although investment clubs aren't for everyone, they can be a useful source of information and education for the individual investor.

## NATIONAL ASSOCIATION OF INVESTORS CORPORATION

Investment clubs generally aren't phony pyramids or other schemes created for an investor to "get rich quick." The National Association of Investors Corporation (NAIC), for one, is a not-for-profit organization devoted to assisting individual investors form and operate investment clubs. Currently there are more than 25,571 clubs that are members of the NAIC, with around 298,213 total members. Here are some interesting statistics from the NAIC:

- Average NAIC member personal portfolio: $388,000.
- Average NAIC investment club total assets: $86,700.

- NAIC member median household income: $114,000.
- Estimated total portfolio value (all NAIC members): $116 billion.
- Total monthly deposits (all NAIC members): $100 million.
- Membership demographics: 67 percent female, 33 percent male; 74 percent hold a college or advanced graduate degree.
- Average investment club age: four years; median age of NAIC members is 55.8.
- Individual investment clubs by gender: 54 percent female, 8 percent male, 38 percent mixed.
- Investment clubs' average size: 11 members investing $84/month; the average investment club commits $927 to common stocks monthly.
- NAIC Top 100 Index: 10-year annual performance (ending December 2002) was 8.8 percent.
- NAIC 110 regional chapters have over 2,000 volunteers holding investment seminars, workshops, computer events, and Investor Fairs across the country throughout the year.

## CONTACT INFORMATION

Address:
National Association of Investors Corporation
711 West Thirteen Mile Road
Madison Heights MI 48071
Phone Toll Free: 1-877-ASK-NAIC (275-6242)
Online: www.better-investing.org
E-mail: service@better-investing.org
Fax: 248-583-4880.

The NAIC provides services and advice for individual investors and investment clubs. The organization also has a low-cost stock purchase plan to facilitate members' purchase of common stock. Some clubs have been in operation for 40 years, and today the majority of investment clubs that belong to NAIC do better with their portfolios than the Standard & Poor's 500 Index.

## HOW DOES A CLUB FUNCTION?

Most clubs have simple rules that can be changed as necessary. Usually, groups of 10 to 20 people, often organized as a legal partnership (for tax purposes), meet on a regular basis, such as monthly. Club officers are elected and members are asked to actively participate through the following activities:

1. Attending the monthly meeting
2. Making a monthly contribution, often a $20 minimum, with no maximum
3. Researching and following the progress of a specific company's stock or a group of stocks that the club owns or has targeted for investment

Based on its strategy, the club invests money in the stock market and normally has one or two members authorized to place trades with a stockbroker. Each member has shares of the investment portfolio, depending on the amount of money he or she contributed (i.e., the $20 monthly minimum and any other contributions).

With a low monthly minimum, virtually anyone can afford to belong to the club. From then on, the main requirements are a willingness to work, learn, and get along with other members. Obviously, a mutually agreed upon system of resolving differences is necessary.

## In Business Together

Since the club is a legal partnership, all the members are effectively in business with each other, with all the advantages and problems that can engender. Trust is essential. The organization sets broad goals of education, to learn about investing in the stock market, capital gains, and making a profit. Club members need to understand that gains can be minimal or even nonexistent for the first couple of years. Often, clubs place restrictions on early withdrawals. Eventually, club members start their own individual portfolios, supported with the knowledge and skills they learned by being an investment club member.

# FEDERAL TAXES

Here's a brief summary of some of the Internal Revenue Service's tax requirements for investment clubs:

## Identifying Number

Each club must have an *employer identification number* (EIN) to use when filing its return. The club's EIN also may have to be given to the payer of dividends or other income from investments recorded in the club's name. If your club does not have an EIN, obtain Form SS-4, "Application for Employer Identification Number," from your nearest

Social Security Administration office, or call 1-800-TAX-FORM (1-800-829-3676). Mail the completed Form SS-4 to the Internal Revenue Service Center where you file the club's tax return.

### Tax Treatment of the Club

Generally, an investment club is treated as a partnership for federal tax purposes, unless it chooses otherwise. In some situations, it can be taxed as a corporation or a trust.

## INVESTMENT CLUBS AND THE SEC?

Investment clubs usually do not have to register themselves or register the offer and sale of their membership interests with the SEC. But since each investment club is unique, each group should explore, examine, and decide if it needs to register in compliance with securities laws.

Two laws can relate to investment clubs:

1. Under the Securities Act of 1933, membership interests in the investment club may be securities. If so, the offer and sale of membership interests could be subject to federal regulations.
2. Under the Investment Company Act of 1940, an investment club may be an investment company, and regulated accordingly.

## STATES REGULATIONS

State securities laws can differ from federal securities laws. To learn more about the laws in your state, call your state securities regulator. Look under state listings in the telephone book, or to get the phone number for your state regulator, call the North American Securities Administrators Association (NASAA) at 202-737-0900, or visit their Web site at www.nasaa.org.

## FOR FURTHER INFORMATION

Call 1-800-SEC-0330 for more information or to request other publications for investors. Publications include *Invest Wisely: Advice from Your Securities Industry Regulators*; a copy of federal securities laws, such as the Investment Company Act of 1940; and the investment company registration package, which contains more information about exceptions to the laws.

You can access the SEC's Web site at www.sec.gov.

## TRUST RESULTS, BUT AUDIT THEM

Obviously, trust is important, but also establish the club with safeguards to protect both the investors and those in charge of the money. As much as possible, remove the opportunity for mistrust; decrease the temptation; make it difficult for someone to walk off with the money. Also, establish a system to ensure that the investment policy and decisions are being followed.

## SUCCESS IS IN THE SETUP

The most difficult thing for a group of people to do is make a decision. Because the initial setup is so important to the successful operation of a club, remove or moderate the decision-making process by relying on experience. Contacting an organization like the NAIC for their suggestions accomplishes much of the difficult organizational work and simplifies the decision process.

# Index

## ABOUT THE AUTHOR

**Michael D. Sheimo** has extensive experience as a registered representative and registered options principal, working at the full-service retail level for Merrill Lynch and Olde Financial Corporation. He is an internationally recognized expert on the Dow Theory and has had books published in India, Malaysia, Korea, China, and Japan.